CRASHED
AND BYRNED

TOMMY BYRNE WITH MARK HUGHES

CRASHED AND BYRNED

THE GREATEST RACING DRIVER YOU NEVER SAW

ICON BOOKS

Published in the UK in 2008 by
Icon Books Ltd, The Old Dairy,
Brook Road, Thriplow,
Cambridge SG8 7RG
email: info@iconbooks.co.uk
www.iconbooks.co.uk

Sold in the UK, Europe, South Africa and Asia
by Faber & Faber Ltd, 3 Queen Square,
London WC1N 3AU or their agents

Distributed in the UK, Europe, South Africa and Asia
by TBS Ltd, TBS Distribution Centre, Colchester Road,
Frating Green, Colchester CO7 7DW

This edition published in Australia in 2008
by Allen & Unwin Pty Ltd,
PO Box 8500, 83 Alexander Street,
Crows Nest, NSW 2065

Distributed in Canada by
Penguin Books Canada,
90 Eglinton Avenue East, Suite 700,
Toronto, Ontario M4P 2YE

ISBN: 978-184831-028-5

Typesetting and design by Simmons Pugh Ltd

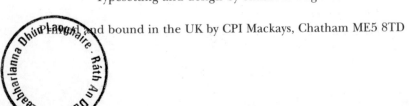 and bound in the UK by CPI Mackays, Chatham ME5 8TD

CONTENTS

ABOUT THE AUTHORS 8

FOREWORD 9

PREFACE 11

PART ONE: ESCAPE

Chapter One
Culchey 15

Chapter Two
The Tale Of The Black Reek 29

Chapter Three
Respect 35

Chapter Four
Crawford 49

PART TWO: UP THE LADDER

Chapter Five
Formula Ford 57

Chapter Six
Ayrton Senna 81

Chapter Seven
I'm The Man, Me And Stan 91

Chapter Eight
Knacker to F1 in Four Years 105

PART THREE: DOWN THE SNAKES

Chapter Nine
The McLaren Test 115

Chapter Ten
Travelling Backwards, Looking West 127

Chapter Eleven
The Clown's Bitch 147

Chapter Twelve
An American Family 155

Chapter Thirteen
The Rock Star And The Undercover Cop 171

Chapter Fourteen
Down, Down Mexico Way 175

Chapter Fifteen
Letting Go 187

Dedicated to my twin sisters Ruby and Pearl.
A special thank you to Michele for taking such
good care of mine and our kids.

ABOUT THE AUTHORS

TOMMY BYRNE was the 1980 Double British Formula Ford 1600 champion, the 1981 British Formula Ford 2000 champion and also the European Formula Ford 2000 champion. In 1982 – having also become British F3 champion – he entered F1, but by the following year had disappeared without trace.

MARK HUGHES is one of sport's top journalists. His books on F1 include the critically acclaimed *Lewis Hamilton: The Full Story* (Icon, 2007), and *Speed Addicts*, which won the 2005 Illustrated Sports Book of the Year.

FOREWORD

How do you sum up Tommy Byrne? **CHARACTER** in big bold letters doesn't even get close to it. Eddie Irvine used to be called the 'character' of F1. Multiply that by ten and you might be getting close to Tommy.

He is the most naturally talented driver I have ever had the pleasure of working with – and I have worked with many. The things he could do with a car most drivers – including several Grand Prix winners and world champions – could only dream about. He could wring the neck of any car in any condition.

When he did get his chance at the big time, Formula One wasn't ready for him. But he was certainly ready for Formula One. His test for McLaren was stunning, but driving for a small run-down team like Theodore was always going to be a tough call. If he had come along ten years later we'd now be counting the Grand Prix wins and probably world championships too.

Tommy came from nothing and achieved a hell of a lot. No, he never really made the big time and the big money. But he was not from the genetically modified personality mould that we see today's drivers pop up from. He had to do it by talent, determination and debt, he didn't suffer fools gladly, said what he thought and if you didn't like it – well that's just the way it was.

Rough around the edges, his story is one of rough-and-tumble against big odds. He's a unique character and I'm very proud to have worked with him and still have him as a true friend. I still get a good laugh at the memories his story brings back. If only we could turn the clock back and do it again. Actually, he probably wouldn't have done it any differently.

Gary Anderson, F1 designer

PREFACE

The story's been a while coming. I've wanted to tell everything for a while but telling it how it was, well it was always going to cause some upset. For example, some won't be impressed by the story of all the whores in Mexico in my friend Orchio's office. One day he went crazy. Coked up to his eyeballs and with the pressures of a million terrible secrets coming back to roost, he pulled a gun on them. Then he shot at me and missed. That's when I decided to get out of Mexico. Two weeks later Orchio was dead at 40 years old, leaving his bitch of a widow with 40 million dollars.

How come it's always me who ends up with these weirdos? I only wanted to get out of Dundalk, yet twenty years later it had come to this ...

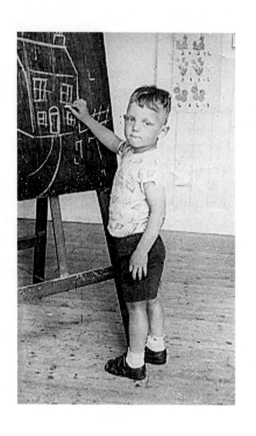

PART ONE:

Escape

CHAPTER ONE

Culchey

Silverstone, October 1982

The helmeted racing driver sits in the F1 McLaren in the pitlane, receiving final instructions from the engineer. This is Tommy Byrne's big chance, the opportunity to prove to the world what only he and a select few motor racing connoisseurs know: that he is the most devastatingly talented driver of his generation. This is a prize test, for winning – make that dominating – the junior category, F3, that is the forming ground for future world champions. It's also a chance for the McLaren team to appraise him. If he could find a way in here, he'd be an instant sensation. He was ready.

God, he'd come so far, so fast. Seemed only yesterday that bastard Crawford laughed at the very idea.

O'Connell Street, Dublin, 1978

A blue Peugeot 504 threads its way through the traffic, the chauffeur twenty years old, lithe, wiry, full of piss and vinegar, the eyes betraying the anger, lips tight shut as he struggles to hold back. Tommy.

The car's owner, Crawford O'Scott – disabled millionaire meat buyer eccentric, a Protestant who'd converted to Catholicism to marry Ramona – is laughing like he's going to have a seizure.

'A fuckin' racing driver? A professional he says? You? Ya daft bollocks, bastard shit fuck boy. Do you need to sniff glue to come up with bollocks like that or do yi think of it all yeself? A race car driver ...'

The laughter stops, a deep frown of concern upon Crawford's face. His bowels ... they're on the move again.

'Boy, stop the car!'

Fuck it. I've had it with this bastard. Fuckin' cripple can find someone else to wipe his arse, clean up all the shite after he's exploded in his pants again. Fuck you Crawford.

'I said stop the car fuck shit bastard boy.'

'I'm sorry Crawford. No can do.'

'Pull the fuckin' car over or I'm going to shit ...'

The sound – blooooooooooooostthuuulssht – the appalling smell. Finally I pull the car over ...

'Sorry about that Crawford ...'

... and climb out, walk away, leaving the swearing, shit-filled, mean-spirited old cripple helpless in the passenger seat of the Peugeot.

I walked back to the bus station in the rain with not even the money to buy my fare back to Dundalk. But no way was I ever going to be changing his shitty pants again after that. That was it. It seemed to be one big feckin' joke, me – the knacker from Dundalk – becoming a racing driver. Well we'd see. From the first time I'd paid my 25 punts and taken that old Formula Ford for a spin around Mondello Park, I knew I'd been given something here – my ticket out of Dundalk.

Well, Dundalk's glorifying it a little actually. Dundalk was the town but we were 'culcheys' – rednecks – living at Blackrock, about six miles away out in the sticks. Nothing much happened up there except farming. It was a bit of a seaside resort and I had some great summer days on the beach. We didn't farm. Mama had a job at the local hotel, Dad at the shoe factory. Combined income once Dad had been to the pub on Tuesday night, Wednesday night, Thursday night, Friday night plus Sunday after Mass but not Sunday or Monday nights: not very much with six kids to look after. Dad would give Mama the cash each week from his wages – but not all of it. It turned out he had a raise from about ten years earlier and had kept it secret from her. I remember the day she found out.

She was waiting for him as he came home from the pub. He was at a bit of a disadvantage, being drunk. I was in bed waiting for my Cadbury's chocolate that he used to bring home for us. The shit hit the fan as she hit him with a teapot full of hot tea as soon as he got in the door. Then came the screaming, swearing and shouting. I realised pretty quick there probably wasn't going to be any Cadbury's that night.

I can still picture us being taken to Mass each Sunday at Haggerstown, about two miles away. We had no car until I was about fourteen, so we would have to walk down the main Dundalk–Dublin road, Dad in front on his own, then Mama with all six kids. We'd be lined up on the road, like ducks in a row. Didn't matter if it was raining, snowing whatever, we'd still be there, cursing under our breath, cursing the weather, cursing Mass, cursing God, cursing Mama after she'd whacked me across the head for cursing, cursing this shitty road as cars whizzed by us, 'rich bastard in your feckin' car'. Cursing ducks all in a row.

The house was later burned down, which led to the family being separated for quite a few months. My mother and three of my sisters – Cynthia, who was about five, the twins, Catrina and Margaret, who were about three – were at the house one day and the twins were asking for sausages. Mama didn't have any in so she jumped on the bike, leaving Cynthia in charge, and headed for Blackrock, about fifteen minutes away. As she was coming back she saw a plume of smoke from over the hill. As she got closer she saw it was coming from our house. The girls were outside with Michael McGeough, a local farmer who'd been out in the field behind the house when he saw the smoke. He'd got the girls out through the front window, for sure saving their lives.

For years it was believed that the fire had started because my pissy blankets were drying near the Rayburn – I always used to wet the bed. I did until I was about sixteen. I remember lying in bed all night cold and wet and I recall talking to a kid at school and noticing he smelt of piss and I thought, 'Oh, he must wet the bed too,' but thinking back, the smell was probably coming from me. It meant I could never stay at anyone else's house and for years if ever I made my sisters or brother mad they'd call me 'piss-the-bed'.

But it turned out the fire was nothing to do with my pissy blankets. It was only much later, at mother's funeral, that Cynthia told me what had really happened. She'd been playing with matches in the kitchen and had started it. She blocked it out until the therapy of the years allowed her to remember it. Unfortunately, Cynthia spent a lot of depressed years over that episode. After the fire we had nowhere to live and we were broken up for a while. Cynthia was sent to Dublin. At five years old, she might as well have been sent to Africa.

A few years later, when I was about ten, a brand-new house was being built across the road from us. I was looking around it one day, looking to see if there was anything to pilfer, when I suddenly got a case of the shits and had to drop my pants right there. I was just in the middle of doing this when I heard a car approaching and I had to take off mid-shite. I was just heading out the house as the owner was heading in. Every time I saw that neighbour for years afterwards I had to look the other way because I knew that he knew I'd shat in his house.

Anyway, Mama and Dad had a job keeping up with what we were up to, me especially. I hated school, hated the idea of being told what to do – still do. I spent very little time there and of course when I did go I struggled, so I assumed I was thick. Turned out later in life I wasn't at all. Stupid maybe, but certainly not thick.

I got beat by Master McGlynn nearly every day at that school, for not doing homework or not listening. He'd have the class taking turns at reading and suddenly I'd hear his voice: 'Continue Mr Byrne.' Oh fuck, I'd think. I'd been in la-la land as usual and of course would be out by a couple of pages. 'Come up here Mr Byrne.' Here we go again. I'd stand there with my hand out while he got his 3-foot-long piece of wood, rolling his sleeves up, salivating because he was getting to inflict some pain. Whack, whack, whack, three on each hand. Sometimes I'd pull my hand away when he was on the downswing and he'd hit his shin – and that just made him madder. I'd walk back with half the class laughing at me, including the school bully, who'd be looking for me at lunchtime. Fuck yeah, I hated school.

I also got whacked by McGlynn once after stealing the money from 'the black babies box'. Everyone in Ireland at that time knew what a 'back babies box' was. The church would collect for the starving in Africa and the schools would collect on the church's behalf too – and the money was put in the black babies box. Well, when I was about ten, me and a friend found the black babies box at school and we stole what was in there – about six pennies. We shared it out, took three pennies each. The other kid told his brother, who then snitched on us. We got whacked for it, but the school also told the father at the church. And for the next two weeks I was shitting myself because I knew he would be around at our house to tell my Ma and Pa, and I was sure I was in for another whacking.

I'd delay getting home for as long as possible, dreading the priest being on the doorstep. And each night, he wasn't there I'd be relieved. But then the worry would creep upon me, because it just meant I had it still to come. Eventually, after about two weeks, there was a knock at the door one night and sure enough it was him. I tried to escape but there was nowhere to go and I was listening in the hallway.

'Hello father.'

'Hello Mrs Byrne, how are you this evening?'

'Fine father. What brings you here?'

'Ah well, there's something I need to talk to you about. Can I come inside?'

'Surely, father.'

And in he comes, mother showing him to the only room in the house that was kept tidy – the front room. They were in there for an agonisingly long time. Then he left. Mother came in. 'So you've taken from the black babies box have you Tommy?'

'Yes well, sort of. It was the other guy's fault.'

I didn't get a second beating but the two weeks of waiting was worse than any beating.

Out-of-school-time was what it was about for me – and getting back to Blackrock let me get onto the tractor. I was only eight or nine when I started hanging about at Pete Murphy's farm. It was just down the road from our house. I liked the farm because of the tractors. Pete had two. They were old grey Massey Ferguson 20s. So at nine years old I'd be out steering one of them in low walking pace gear digging up the turnips as the others picked them.

After that I would always try to get in position to be the one called to steer the tractor – because there were others kids as well. Pete used to get all the local kids to help him for free. A lot of them came and went but I always stayed, rain, shine, snow, sleet or frost. I stayed so long – about five years – that I actually started to get paid half a crown a month in 1968. When Pete gave me the half-crown he would slip it into my hand and say, 'Don't spend it all in the same shop.' And I would always think it wouldn't be hard to spend it in one shop – tight bastard. I was getting the same half-crown for four years, but loved the farm so much I would have worked there for free.

As soon as I got home from school I would head straight off there. No homework. My mother and my Dad were working so there was no one to tell me to do my homework. And if they did I would just say I had done it. So my grades were not so good – Fs and Ds, whack-whack-whack.

Friday was my favourite day, especially in the summer, because that was when we would be cutting the hay and the corn and we would work in the field sometimes till eleven o'clock at night. I loved those long summer days on the farm, getting the hay cut and baled while the weather was still dry.

I can still hear the cutting machine on the back of the Ferguson with the blades going. They used to jam up early in the morning with the dew. We spent more time unjamming the fucking thing than actually cutting. Then, when it did cut, every half-day we would have to sharpen each blade with a fine file – and there were about twenty blades with two sides to sharpen. Sometimes we had to replace certain blades – very unproductive. From what I remember, 50 per cent of the working day was spent fixing shit.

Pete had hired a guy called Gerry, who was a bit older than me – maybe sixteen or seventeen – to do most of the work. He was my main man. I never knew where he lived or what he did when he was at home, or whether he had brothers, sisters, uncles, aunts. Just that I would be sitting there waiting for him every morning and he would pull up on his motorcycle – an old Guigley 20, the one that you had to pedal to start. He was my best friend because he let me drive the tractors a lot, plus he had a motorcycle.

When the hay was cut you would leave it on the ground for a couple of weeks. Then, when it turned brown, it was time to bale it into squares – so it was time to bring out the baler. It was called a 'New Holland' but there was nothing new about it. That piece of shite broke down constantly. Whenever it jammed up they would have me climb in the back of it and crawl inside the guts of the thing. I'd go in there and push the hay out of this little hole in the side. The moment it was all cleared, Gerry would shout, 'OK, start her up!' – the bastard. I'd be shouting, 'No, no you fuckers!' and as he started the engine I'd be scrabbling backwards in the darkness, banging my arms, elbows and head, 'No, no please!' Then I'd get out and they'd all be laughing their heads off – bastards.

As you might gather, I had quite a vocabulary for a ten-year-old. The farm taught me to swear, listening to farmers curse all day long, usually at cows or sheep or pigs – 'Get up ya cunt-ya, go on ya hurs, get up there ya bastard'. When Pete was grabbing the balls of the bullocks, ready to castrate them, he'd be saying, 'Ah, you're going to love this, how do you like that, you fucker.'

The routine with the combine and me inside it was just one of the ways I'd be tortured there. Another favourite was to hang me from the top of the haystack by one leg. I'd be screaming blue murder, convinced they were going to drop me, 'Please let me down, I will never fuck with you again, wah, wah. Please, please ...' until they let me go then I would turn around and give them the fingers: 'Fuck off ye's bastards!' and I'd be safe for the time being – until they caught me again.

Pete's tractors were not powerful enough for the

New Holland, so he used to borrow the Massey Ferguson 25 from his brother Mick Murphy. I loved that tractor. It had a throttle pedal by your right foot just like a car, plus it had six speeds, high and low ratios, and it was red and it had a key, which Pete's tractors did not.

Before you baled the hay you had to get it into neat rows. There would be somebody raking, somebody baling, then we would be coming behind with the tractor and picking up the bales. I would be driving, then there would be two guys lifting the bales onto the trailer and one building the bales like blocks. This was the most important job because sometimes it would be 20 feet high and it had to be driven a mile back to the farm – which felt like 20 miles – and if they were not properly stacked the load would fall off halfway. When the load reached about 20 feet, knitted together there perfectly, the two ropes were thrown from front to back and tied down. I would climb up on the top for the ride back to the farm. It was like I was on top of the world. Everybody waved at you when you were on the top of the world like that. I liked that. I felt like I was someone. I waved back – and sometimes gave them the two fingers, depending who it was.

That defiance, that troubling but appealing mix of vulnerability and cockiness, was all there as Tommy stood atop that haystack giving the fingers to any he didn't like. This was the world as Tommy felt it should have been, but wouldn't ever be: with him on top.

This was the fantasy that any kid brought up as a runt in a big litter might indulge himself in. Lack of parental interest in his education, lots of siblings, not enough money to support any of them, a dead-end world where adults couldn't care less and other kids bullied – it's difficult not to see the ten-year-old Tommy as an incidental accident of Catholic beliefs on birth control. Little wonder he loved it up there on top of the wagon.

He was the fourth child of six, with four sisters – including twins – and an older brother. He was born on 6 May 1958 in a car speeding down Tullystea hill, trying to get to Droheda hospital in time. After the birth, his aunt wrapped him in her scarf. Many years later Tommy asked his mother who the car belonged to, as the family didn't have a car, and who was driving it. She told him she couldn't remember. But he got the feeling, even then, that everything about the past was a big secret. He's always rebelled against that secrecy. Tommy Byrne remains painfully open, sometimes like a raw wound.

My farming days were over when Pete and his wife went to a wedding one day. My brother Peter and I got the two tractors running and we were racing them around the yard in circles. That was my first oval racing experience! We were having a great time until Pete came home early and caught us: 'Go home ya fuckers.'

Tommy's maternal grandmother, Nana Kelly, was once shot at by the British when she was halfway up a pole trying to hang a tricolour from her house at a time of particular political tension. She hated the British with a passion.

She was a big, mean woman. She was married to someone always referred to in the family as 'auld man Kelly', who I never met. He ran away when my mother was still a baby. I often found myself being compared to auld man Kelly. That wasn't considered a good thing. That much was made clear by the way it was said through narrowed eyes and clenched teeth. But if you'd known my Granny, you wouldn't have blamed auld man Kelly for running away. He ran off to England somewhere and started another family. My sister Rita knows something about that because I used to hear her and my Great-Aunt Tessie talk about it sometimes, when they were having a few brews. But that's a secret. Because auntie didn't drink! She hid the drink away from Granny for years. But even after Granny was dead, she still hid the fuckin' drink!

Anyway my Granny was a very angry woman, and so was my mother. She'd been brought up in 1920s Ireland with no father. You can imagine the stigma of that. It certainly left its mark on her. She was embittered – with good reason. She tried hard to look after us, she really did her best. But there wasn't enough money to go around, she had to work hard just to get what little there was – and she didn't get a lot of help from Dad – and we were a handful, me especially. I'd defy anyone under the same circumstances to do better. All she wanted was to own her own sweetshop one day.

She was the boss. My father was no threat to her. They met at some dance in Blackrock. I don't think it was love so much as 'get the hell out of the house' because Dad was still living with his mother at thirty, ten years older than my mother while Mama was still living with Nana Kelly. He drank five nights a week, she was teetotal and angry. I never really got to know his family, as they were from Dundalk, six miles away. When our house burned down I went to live with his sisters, pissing in their bed every night. It was very embarrassing. My Dad never hit my mother, but I saw her hit him plenty of times. He never answered her back, unless he'd had a few. Then there'd be a huge fight.

The secrecy thing is all to do with Irish attitudes about sex. It's clothed in guilt. I had my first sexual experience at fourteen, with my friend's twelve-year-old sister, Maureen. I stuck it in and after about three strokes I felt faint and had to stop. I looked down and there was stuff coming out of me. I didn't like it. So much for all the hype my friends had been giving me. The girl went and told her brother everything, including me almost fainting after just a few seconds. Some time later the brother says to me, 'Listen, I don't mind you doing my sister. Everybody else does.' I said 'OK, but I'm not ever going to do that stuff again. It sucks.' Her brother and his friend burst out laughing. Anyway, I soon changed my mind and next time I was with Maureen I managed to go a lot longer before feeling faint – maybe about five strokes this time! But now, I decided, I liked it. Maureen was very willing and we did it a lot over the next few months, but then she and her wacko family moved to Belfast and that was the end of sex for me for a long time.

We were told sex was a vile, dirty, filthy act – only to be done for the making of babies. You succumbed to it and asked for forgiveness afterwards. You couldn't buy rubbers in the chemist – because they were illegal. You would've had to go over the border in Northern Ireland, and you'd get a friend to get them for you – otherwise everyone in the shop would know you were having vile dirty sex. That's why I'm not the only Irishman who has an English offspring. The girls would go over to England – either for an abortion or to give birth – without anyone in Ireland knowing. The baby would then be brought up by English friends or relatives or put up for adoption. There are some heartbreaking tales along those lines. The Catholic faith has certainly led to a lot of very fucked-up Irish families.

When mother died, a girl came to the funeral from England. She was the daughter of one of my aunts – mother's sister. The girl came with the intention of comforting auntie but the embarrassment was just too much for my aunt, and she completely ignored this girl – made like she didn't even know who she was. A few years later, when auntie died, her English daughter didn't come to the funeral and instead said: 'I hope she rots in hell.' The world is full of bastard Irish kids.

One of them walked into my life 21 years after he'd been born. I was at the Texas Motor Speedway and I got a phone call from my ex, Caroline. I knew straight-away what it was about. She told me she'd got in touch with Jeff and did I want to be part of his life. Of course I did. Since then I've had only good times with Jeff. He's a great kid and was brought up by a great English couple, who I'm so grateful to.

Jeff is a little like me with all his crazy ideas and attention deficit disorder – and how he will not listen to anybody. But we get along like brothers. He was brought up with another adopted kid, Matt, who came to visit me as well, and we had a great time together.

CHAPTER TWO

The Tale Of The Black Reek

I just loved driving. No idea where it came from, it was just the one thing that brought some joy into my life at that time. I remember when I was four or five years old I got one of those pedal cars for Christmas – the ones that you never could pedal. I would have my brother push me all over the place. Then, when it was his turn for me to push, I usually only lasted a few minutes then I would convince him to push some more. That's my first memory of driving.

So when I discovered that Tony Sharkey – a brick-layer who lived in Blackrock – had a stock car racing Mini, I wanted to be in on the act. From about the age of fourteen, and for about the next three years, I became his helper; and when I wasn't tear-arsing under-age around the roads, I was helping Tony. I got my first shitty job during this time too, but I'll tell you about that later. This is much more interesting.

Irish stock car racing wasn't a scene for shrinking violets. A cast of lairy characters straight out of, or on their way into, institutions, a side order of intimidation, the smell of fried onions from the burger van mingling with that of petrol and mud, the sound of racing engines muffled by the grass as the cars were readied. And an undercurrent of The Troubles.

Tony had a head of bright red hair, a fierce temper and loved to fight. He was the best bricklayer in Ireland, could get as much work as he could handle and, like a lot of people in Blackrock, he struggled with the drink. You meet a lot of supposed hard men but Tony was the most fearless bastard I ever met. I've seen him tell a man with a gun at a checkpoint – a man that could have been with any one of a number of terrorist groups – to 'Get out of my fuckin' face, will ya,' not knowing or caring who he was, just knowing that he wanted to be on his way. This was scary behaviour at this place at this time. He just did not give a fuck.

We'd trail this Mini from Dundalk – where he raced at Oriel Park, around the outside of the soccer field – up to County Armagh, scary bandit country in the north. He'd crash the car nearly every night and I'd weld it back together the next day.

We built it up ourselves, took out the interior, stripped it, welded bars underneath. We thought it was the dog's bollocks but it must've weighed a ton and was a complete piece of shite really. Up north was where people knew how to build cars: instead of using 4x4 quarter-inch box iron for the frame they were using inch and a quarter, and when they crashed their cars they fixed them properly and then repainted, where we just beat ours out with a sledgehammer. We were complete culcheys (rednecks) and I was the biggest one of all.

Tony never did any good with that car in Northern Ireland so he decided to buy one of those special ones from up north. This Mini was a beautiful car, 13-inch wheels, a special Cooper S engine with downdraft Weber carburettors, a full race cam. He bought it from a guy called Richard Douglas, from County Armagh, who was a great driver, an autocross champion. We became very friendly with him and would spend three or four nights a week up there – a pretty evil place at that time.

On the way there from Dundalk was especially scary for a young Catholic boy, because at that time there were a lot of killings of Catholics by the UDA (Ulster Defence Association) dressed in RUC (Royal Ulster Constabulary) uniforms and we used to get stopped at least three times each way. This was at the height of the Troubles and you didn't want to be travelling up north with a southern-registered car. Who was stopping you this time? UVF, UDA, UFF? Sometimes you even got stopped by the IRA or if it wasn't them it was the Brits (soldiers).

This was about the same time as the Miami show-band killings, when members of a cabaret band from the south, returning in their minibus after performing in Belfast, were flagged down at a bogus army check-point that was really the UVF (Ulster Volunteers Force). The UVF was a banned paramilitary force of Protestants, but many of their members were also part of the Ulster Defence Regiment (the army) and it was like that with these guys. So despite the uniform, you never knew who it really was that was stopping you. While two of the UVF guys questioned the band, another two were attempting to plant a bomb on the bus, the idea being to frame the band as members of the IRA. But as they were doing this, the bomb went off, killing the two UVF guys that were trying to plant it. The remaining UVF guys then opened fire on the band, killing three of them right there on the road.

So I'd be shitting myself, especially on the way back when it was dark and you didn't know who might have seen us leaving Richard's and called us in. And that is how I felt on the way home – always waiting for somebody to stop us around any of the many turns and humps. Not Tony though, he really couldn't have given a fuck.

As if that wasn't scary enough, there was also the manner of his driving on the public road. He went everywhere flat out, but always looked awkward at the wheel. He was right up close to it with a big gap between his back and the back of the seat and when he went round the corner at 100mph he would be half falling out of the seat. There was one turn in particular that I used to dread every time. It was just about flat out but was blind, with a jump in the middle. Every time the Hillman estate – with the trailer and the Mini don't forget – would land on the wrong side of the road and I'd thank my lucky stars there was nothing coming the other way. On any given journey it was only when we'd cleared that turn that I knew I was safe and that we'd get back home again. What with the worry about the bandits as well, these journeys were the scariest shit I've ever done. Forget F1 cars or 200mph on oval tracks.

This new Mini was so much faster than the old one and Tony started to do quite well. We were racing in Portadown one night when he had a bit of a confrontation with the big northern hero, 'The Black Reek'. Just like all the other drivers up north, The Black Reek was a Protestant. He used to put his helmet on with the strap in his mouth. He was a tough customer, very fast, and the crowd loved him, like he was some sort of folk hero. Can't remember another feckin' thing about him. Anyway, in the middle of this dice, he punted Tony off the track. When The Black Reek goes by next lap Tony throws his helmet at him, whacks the side of his car with it. The Black Reek stops, mid-race, and jumps out. Tony stands his ground, starts shouting abuse at him and all hell breaks loose. The crowd get out of their stands, start to invade the track and there's nearly a full-scale riot. The RUC escorted us back to the border that night and every time we raced in Portadown after that.

I got to race one night when Tony got injured. He'd been flying in the first heat but then suddenly was in the fence up on his side. Luckily he was not injured at this point and started climbing out through the window. Just as he was half-out, The Black Reek came flying around the corner and T-boned him, breaking Tony's collarbone. The crowd loved it and there was never any question of The Black Reek being penalised or punished – this was his territory, Protestant territory, and us couple of ragamuffin Catholics from the South had some sort of a nerve even being there.

But no way was Tony going home just for the sake of a broken collarbone. He told me to drive the car in the final. I was only too happy to oblige. As I got in to buckle up I looked down at the bottom of the steering rack and remembered the bolt that I had borrowed from there the week before for my own Mini and obviously I had forgotten to put it back. 'Hah,' I thought, 'so that's how he ended in the fence!' I was able to replace it before Tony found out – and he did not find out until years later, when it was safe to tell him. If he'd known at the time he would have beat the shit out of me.

Anyhow, here I was, about to do my first race in the wet on an oval and on the pole (because the grid was slowest first and obviously Tony hadn't finished the previous heat). Well, I was shitting myself because I had never driven a Mini like this. All I could hear was the screaming of The Black Reek's engine five cars behind me, but in the race I was too busy trying to keep my car on the track to be thinking about The Black Reek as he drove by me as if I were stopped. Then the race was over and I finished about fourth. I'd just been starting to get the hang of it.

Tony was a good friend of mine, was very good to me and helped me a lot, taking me everywhere, and my mother liked him a lot too – and there weren't too many people she liked. I'd left Ireland and was racing in England when Tony quit the stock cars and went back to the drink. He lost everything, including his wife, and he ended up living on the streets. Years later he got on the wagon, got his house back and got plenty of bricklaying work again.

But I was visiting back from England one day and driving down the road when I saw a red-haired figure walking by the side – Tony. He was a tramp. I took him to my Ma's place, got him bathed. He was a mess – full of lice – but he wouldn't let me get rid of these horrible old dirty clothes and was trying to put them back on. My mother convinced him to put some of my Dad's old clothes on and he took his other ones with him in a plastic bag.

CHAPTER THREE

Respect

So there I'm standing, waiting my turn in the racing school's car at Mondello racetrack, having handed over my 25 punts for 25 laps. I'd been driving cars around on the roads underaged for years, but now, at seventeen, I was old enough to have a car licence, so I was old enough to go to the race school.

As well as driving cars, I also had a motorbike. Car or bike, I could not go slow, I was incapable of going slowly. Everywhere I went was flat out – 85mph back to 0 from the very first day I got the bike. People were begging me to get rid of it and later, when I came to have kids myself, I realised the worry I must've caused. Everybody could hear me coming at two in the morning, flat out with no exhaust muffler. I'd take it to 85mph on the Dundalk–Dublin road, hold it flat out with my stomach over the petrol tank until I came to my braking point, then bang the gears down, blipping the throttle, then lay it over hard for the left-hander into our road, shifting my weight back to the right as there was a sort of little chicane there. I'd accelerate back up to about 60 before I'd have to brake for our house. I'd stay on the back brake a little longer than the front so I could slide the back end around our front gate. Then I'd ride to the back of the house, put the front tyre up against the back door, lean forward and open the door, then ride into the hallway and shut it off. What a little bastard. And usually drunk.

It was a spring day in 1976 at Mondello and it was pissing down. I was no more fucked up than any other seventeen-year-old brought up in Catholic Ireland in tough circumstances. Well, maybe I was, I'm not sure. At the time I thought it was normal that you'd get beatings off your family – whether that was Dad when he was drunk or my mother slapping me hard across the face for some misdemeanour or other.

I had a plan to get out and this day at Mondello was the start of it. Actually, I'd never have been standing there if it wasn't for the fact that I'd been sacked from my first job for stealing. I'm not excusing myself: I did steal. I'd been pilfering since I was a kid. I used to rob from the shops in Blackrock and once I just happened to be leaning against the cellar door of a pub there and it opened – so I walked in and took a crate of Guinness, which me and my mate took to the sand dunes. There we had a Guinness-drinking competition. I think I'd got to about fourteen before I started puking. I was shitting black for a week afterwards. I've never touched Guinness since.

Anyway, word got back to Ma somehow, and she was

waiting for me when I got home. 'Sergeant Igio's been to the house, has told me all about what you've been up to. He knows everything. Now you're going to come with me to the police station and own up and he will see what he can do to keep you out of jail.' I was shitting myself so I spilled my guts out to him when we got there. 'That's very interesting, thank you,' he said and gave me an almighty bollocking. Turned out he'd known nothing about it – I'd been conned by my Ma.

But I still had this thing for pilfering. It was like a disease. I got my first job as an apprentice mechanic at an engineering company called CRV in Dundalk. That's where I learned to weld. I started making stuff and taking it home. Usually this would be considered stealing but at CRV it was called pilfering – and I was very good at it. There was a guy called Nixer, who used to do the most take-home jobs, until I came along. The guy I was supposed to be apprenticed to, Pete, was forever shouting for me because I wasn't where I was supposed to be. He used to call me 'foot-and-a-half' because I was so short.

I hung out with a guy called Aidean, also known as 'the murderer's brother', as his brother was doing time for murdering a girl he'd picked up at a club. My uncle John – who, as a friend of the foreman, got me the job there because I didn't have the required school grades – told me not to hang out with Aidean as he would get me in trouble. But I didn't need any help getting in trouble, I could do just fine on my own. I used to hang out with Aidean after work. We worked on cars together – me and another friend of mine could steal an engine from a parked car in about 25 minutes. I figured if a car was parked for more than one day, it was abandoned.

I was out on a roof one day, sunbathing, when I heard voices below me. I shimmied over to the edge to see who it was. It was Aidean and Nixer. They were up to something and I obviously was not included. I couldn't really hear what they were saying but decided to bluff them. I went up to them and said, 'So, you bastards are doing a job without telling me.' They denied it until I told them that I heard everything from the roof.

The heist was truck tyres. They were going to steal ten truck tyres from a big storeroom. We were to go in at night through the railway yard that butted up to the factory. We got dropped off on the top of a bridge by another accomplice in a VW van, the three of us scurried down the embankment to the railway tracks, where we followed them along to the back gates of CRV. Nixer snipped the lock with a big pair of bolt cutters, which we'd pilfered earlier that day from CRV. We snuck all the way back to the storeroom where the tyres were, making sure not to make much noise, in case we alerted the nightwatchman. When we got to the storeroom we snipped that lock as well and started wheeling the tyres out and along the railway track and up the embankment through a wooden gate in the stone wall. These were big truck tyres, bigger than me. I had a hell of a time trying to get my first tyre up the embankment. I had it up three-quarters of the way and I slipped and that fucking tyre ran backward over me and down the embankment and about half a mile away. All I could hear from Aidean and Nixer was 'Ya stupid bollocks, go get it.' Once all the tyres were up by the gate we signalled for the VW to come.

We were there for about three hours in total and I was knackered by the end. I got dropped off at my house and the tyres were gone to some lucky truck owner who I never knew. All I know is my share of the money was 10 punts, but it was not the money, it was the excitement of getting away with it.

That led to more. My most spectacular pilfer was a rolling pulley for taking out engines – which disappeared from 100 feet in the air. I had to lift the cutting equipment into the cockpit of the crane and then move it into position with the crane, then climb up the pulley, which was attached to a big channel steel pole. I cut the pulley down from over 100 feet high and got it stashed away in about ten minutes at lunchtime – very risky stuff. As far as I know, that pulley is still in my old shed in my Ma's old house, working the big sliding door.

It all turned to shite when I bumped into a guy who worked in the upholstery shop. He was telling me he was going into the upholstery business on the outside and what a big help it would be if he was to take some of the makings of the seat home and make what he wanted, but he would never be able to get it out. 'No problem,' I said. 'I can get anything out. Tell me what you want and I'll get it tonight.'

I went and stashed it up behind the big wall. I would come back that night to retrieve it. I had no car at the time so I recruited a friend, Gerry Yore and his Mini. I jumped over the 8-foot wall and started throwing the stuff out to Gerry – four or five rolls of different upholstery. We were at it for no more than a minute, and I was just about to drive away, when four police cars surrounded us. I put my head down, I knew I was fucked.

'So what's your name?'

'Tom Byrne.'

'And what are you doing here?'

'Oooh I was just picking up some stuff that is no good to anybody.'

'And you have permission to take this stuff?'

'Yes, no, well you don't really need permission if it's no good to anybody. They were probably going to throw it out anyhow.'

Well, the garda didn't buy that and we were arrested for thievery. They kept us in there for 24 hours and didn't tell anyone where we were. That was the longest 24 hours I've ever spent. No sleep, people shouting, and of course Detective Prenty wanted to know if I knew about anyone else taking stuff home. I would have to say everybody took stuff home so I didn't tell – even when they asked me about some big truck tyres that had gone missing some months before.

When I got home my parents didn't say a word to me – they didn't have to, I felt bad enough. Then we went to court and I told the judge that Gerry Yore did not know what was happening and what I was up to. He got off and I got a fine and probation and was fired. It made the paper. I met that upholstery guy years later when he was working for my friend Maurice, and he denied ever knowing me. But I wasn't angry. I looked at it this way: if I hadn't got fired I would never have gone racing, and years later, when I was leading two championships in England, they were pleased to see me when I went to visit the CRV factory. The clippings on the wall were of me winning races, not of getting caught stealing. A few years later I stopped stealing things, stopped having the urge to steal, like it was just switched off overnight. Today, if I found $10,000 in a phone box I'd hand it in. I've no idea where the urge came from, even less idea why it suddenly stopped.

Sorry, I sort of got waylaid there didn't I? I was supposed to be telling you about my first run in the racing school car. So eventually my turn came, I got in the car, started it up, crunched the lever into gear and set about becoming a racing driver. I soon found my way around the place, got the hang of the car in a couple of laps really. God it was the easiest thing. Fantastic. Braking as late as I could everywhere, smoke pouring off the tyres. I had a few spins – like about seven in fifteen laps – but I caught the attention of the school's owner, John Murphy.

On the way home that day I knew that I was the best driver ever and that I was going to be a race car driver and make money from that. I had such a buzz I couldn't sleep for a couple of days. It sounds simplistic now but it really did feel like I knew my way out of Dundalk from that day, how I was going to do it. I couldn't begin to describe the excitement of it. I knew it was possible. I'd started reading Autosport and in there were reports of three Irish guys – Derek Daly, David Kennedy and Bernard Devaney – who were doing very well racing in England. And so I figured, if they can make it so can I.

'He was the best of us, by far,' says Devaney of the outstanding Irish contingent of Formula Ford racers of the 1970s.

'For some reason I was always about half-a-step away from Tommy when he raced,' says Daly. 'I had a suspicion that he had great raw talent, but a talent that needed a manager and/or a packager. He seemed a bit like me in the early days, driven by a blind ambition and oblivious to the fact that it was a team sport, and that we needed people support also. I

think I got away with it a little longer than Tommy because he had a more aggressive/curt personality than me.'

Kennedy says: 'I saw him doing things with a racing car that didn't seem possible. He was blessed in a way none of the rest of us were, in a way that maybe only a handful of drivers have ever been. What he had in his hands was a magic that defies description. Ayrton had it, maybe Gilles Villeneuve had it – and Tommy had it. It was something extra.'

Daly, Kennedy and Devaney had got out of Ireland and made their name in England, where it all happened. But first you needed to make your name in Ireland. Tommy didn't have a pot to piss in. The only thing of any value in the family was some land that his mother had inherited, not much more than a field but with some value as building land. Still on a high from his 25 laps at racing school, he talked her into borrowing 2,500 punts against the land so he could buy an old Formula Ford car. The money borrowed against the land was never paid back. Spent on a dream of escape.

With the money, I bought a Formula Ford Crosslé, which I raced, mainly at Mondello for the next few months – my first season of being a racing driver. It was too old to be competitive, but I did better with it than people were expecting, made a bit of an impression. It broke down a lot.

The Irish champion of the time was a guy called Joey Greenan. A very fast and experienced driver, he might have had more of a career if he'd not started so late. One day at Mondello he was leading the race and came to lap the young rookie in the ancient Crossle – and couldn't. 'I didn't know who this guy was,' said Greenan, 'and I could see his car was very slow on the straight, but through the corners he was very quick and he had the most amazing car control I'd ever seen. I could see the rear upright of his car was held on at the top by what looked like coat-hanger wire, it was a real old wreck, but boy could he drive it! He raced me as if it was for the lead, placing his car perfectly. I eventually got past but I'd been hugely impressed. Afterwards I went to the Mondello Racing School and said, 'I've just seen the most amazing new talent.' They asked who and I said this guy Tommy Byrne and they said: 'That eedjit? No.' I was adamant and told them I was going to have him test my Royale at the track the next day and that they should come and watch. He didn't fit the car properly, being much smaller than me, and it was very different to what he'd been driving but straight-away he was within two-tenths of a second of me. They said, 'Jeez, you're right,' and from there they offered him a car for the Formula Ford Festival that year [1977] – and that was a critical part of his early career. There were about 350 drivers in the Festival in those days and Tommy, with just a few months' experience of racing, finished in the top ten, in what was an outdated car.'

It may have been a superb performance in the circumstances but it wasn't going to get him his ticket into British mainstream racing. He continued into 1978 in Ireland, still on a shoestring budget.

I remember once testing at Mondello when the car broke and I just had to wait at the side of the track while the session went on. Standing only about 10 feet away from the cars I was very impressed by two guys – Kenny Acheson and Eddie Jordan. Acheson was in the latest Crosslé Formula Ford and it looked so much faster than mine that I desperately wanted to be in it. Jordan was in a much more powerful Formula Atlantic car with wings and slick tyres, painted up in Marlboro colours. I'd seen him in the paddock and he seemed really 'big time'. Now, as he sped by, I was very impressed. I had no way of knowing that he would later figure in my own career.

Byrne sounds like he was a bad-un, doesn't he? Maurice Roddy, a Dundalk car dealer, was an early mentor of Tommy's. Maurice is solid gold, a 'strong words calmly spoken' sort of guy, about ten years Tommy's senior. He's built up one of the most successful Renault dealerships in Ireland. He saw another side of the bad-ass itinerant pilferer: 'I'd sold his parents a second-hand but perfectly sound Triumph Toledo, which I think was a bit of a stretch for them. Within a year it was absolutely knackered – and it was obvious it had been caned. Tommy had been thrashing up and down the lanes in it. I met him and he told me he was helping Tony Sharkey, who I knew, race the Mini.

'Tommy was a good kid but clearly a bit wayward. His heart was in the right place but I think he'd had a bit of a tough childhood and certainly he was rough around the edges. I liked him – it's very hard not to like Tommy – and would help wherever I could over the years.'

I continued being a culchey even when I'd officially become a racing driver. I used to trail that old Crosslé around in a borrowed knackered old VW van. I'd got a speeding ticket on the way up to Mondello once and then as I came to the track I was waiting to cross it. There wasn't a tunnel or bridge to get into the paddock on the infield. Even with racing cars going round, you would just wait at the side of the track and wait for a gap in the traffic and then just cross. Well, I drove across and didn't the VW go and shit itself and stop in the middle of the track! Just as P.J. Fallon was coming down the hill. He swerved around the van and trailer shaking his fist at me. I gave him the fingers.

In the race, I crashed. Afterwards, I loaded the crashed car onto the blown-up VW and got towed back by my friend Maurice. Although he never raced, Maurice was a brilliant driver, a natural. Well, on the two-hour drive back behind his Morris Marina, we were often nudging 100mph on some of the toughest roads in Ireland. That would've been OK, but for some reason I could hardly steer the van. By the end of the journey my arms were almost hanging off. Then, as I untied the tow rope, I saw I'd tied it around the steering rod!

I then met a guy called Brian Lennox, who owned a petrol station and had formed a race team. He had a FF1600 Hawke and a big bus, and I began driving for him. He tried to teach me how to act professionally and do the right things to get to the top. He got me a job in Dublin, in a body shop run by a friend of his. I'd work all day then go back to an empty flat with just a radio for company.

I was reflecting on all this twenty years later at mother's funeral. Being with my siblings, it all came out about the borrowed money that hadn't been paid back and a whole load of other stuff I thought was long forgotten. I was shocked. I couldn't handle it. I was sick to my stomach, lying here in the same bed as my dead mother had been the night before, afraid to sleep.

I left first thing next morning. I got to reflecting on what could have pissed them all off against me so much. I thought back to our early childhood. I was always able to get what I wanted from my parents if I threw enough of a fuss – and I threw lots of fusses. My parents had nothing to give – but I took it anyway because of my personality. I recall the time I wanted Ma to buy me some spinach because I watched Popeye and I thought if I had some spinach like him, it would stop me getting beat up at school. Ma would go into town every other Saturday and I'd remind her about the spinach before she left – and she was always forgetting and I'd go nuts. Eventually I got my spinach. It was in a can, she opened it, I took one look at it and decided I'd rather get the shite kicked out of me than eat it. This sort of thing went on all the time and I hadn't realised it was pissing off my siblings so much. Then, when you go racing it's normal that everything is given to you and nobody ever tells you when you are wrong. Until you lose everything and the truth comes out.

My racing success and downfall estranged us. See, it's like I had ideas above my station, thinking I could escape and be a big shot. And then, when I fell, they're waiting in line to kick me. Looking back that's how it seems now. It wasn't much different even when I had escaped and was showing the rest of the world what I already knew – that I could do this better than just about anyone's been able to do it. Even then – even as I was having the success, the victories, the new lap records, the championships, climbing the racing ladder – even then, it was like the racing world tolerated me but didn't embrace me, a knacker from Dundalk. Where was the respect? The fuckin' respect, you fuckers!!!

Don't get the idea from this that Tommy carries this anger and frustration around in his normal persona. He absolutely does not. Most of the time he's great fun, an apparently happy-go-lucky little guy with a great line in piss-taking and an even better one in self-deprecation. He's a warm human being, friendly with most people, capable of being a great friend, though capable of bearing a grudge too. His mind is fast and sharp, his wit instant, his charm ready and cheeky and he's often the life and soul of the party. He doesn't stay on one subject long, has a low boredom threshold, but bounces onto the next one with vigour. In his day-job as a race driving instructor at Mid Ohio the pupils tend to love him, the way he can impart his huge knowledge in such a funny way. But when you get him to reflect on how and why he didn't attain his dreams, the anger about respect is there. Respect was the one thing denied him in his upbringing and was the one thing his phenomenal talent should have guaranteed him in the motorsport world. He has a keen antenna – maybe an over-keen one – for any lack of that respect.

In contrast to Tommy's time there, Ireland is now one of the wealthiest countries in Europe in terms of per capita income. With a little help from the EU it has achieved its own economic miracle in the last decade-and-a-half. Blackrock is now a very nice, pretty desirable place to live. Going back there with Tommy, driving in the car, a beautiful coastal picture below the cliff-top road that snakes its way down to the beach, it's easy to imagine this is a scene from a parallel life of Tommy's, where he's succeeded in F1 and is a retired, wealthy, world-renowned legend coming to spend a few months in his Blackrock pad. In this world he's totally at ease with his past. The old tensions, with family and place, have long-since been resolved. The real-time scene from the car, with Tommy still fit and trim and the scenery so beautiful, looks identical to how that parallel scenario would look. Except for a furrow in the brow.

CHAPTER FOUR

Crawford

Anyway, sorry about the rant. I was telling you about my racing career wasn't I? I borrowed the money and bought this old Formula Ford. Then, after a spell driving for Brian Maddox, I traded the Crosslé up for another, better, car – a PRS. There was a guy called Petesy McGeough who became my manager. He was a father of six but wasn't living with his wife and kids on account of she threw him out because he liked his drink – liked a lot of drinks, in fact.

Anyhow, first thing he did for me as a manager was get me a job. He worked in Finnegan's selling tractors and tractor parts. He had the gift of the gab and was a great salesman – those farmers went home with parts they would NEVER use.

Some people moved into the house across the road from Finnegan's and Petesy got talking to them. This was Crawford the millionaire meat buyer and his wife Ramona. As luck would have it they were looking for a chauffeur. 'I just happen to have the man for you,' says Petesy. 'As a matter of fact he's a professional. He even has a race car.'

So Petesy explains about the job – get paid good money for driving this guy around in a brand-new Peugeot. Easy, right? Wrong.

I was to report 6am next morning. I walked up his driveway about 6.30, hung over and met a barrage of abuse: 'Hey boy, have you any idea what the feckin' time is?' 'Hey boy' became his name for me.

'Bastard, fuck, shit, hey boy. Open the door for me.' This was to become second nature because he had some sort of sickness that made him shake when he tried to walk. He said his back hurt as well. So to get him into the car you had to get up behind him, hold him and then kind of lift and coax him all at the same time. The first morning I had some help from Ramona. 'Come on Crawford, you can do it,' she's shouting. He lifted his right leg and tried to put it into the car. He got it up about three-quarters of the way before the pain became too much. 'Come on Crawford,' she repeats. He tries again, gets his foot about a quarter of the way. Again the pain, again Ramona shouting.

'Bastard, fuck shit,' he replied. 'Shut-up, I'm trying.'

What had I got myself into here? This was an odd situation even by the standards of Blackrock. Anyway, we eventually got him into the car. The seat had to be tilted all the way back on account of his bad back, with the result that he couldn't see much of the road – or the speedometer. Off we went north to Belfast, to Tunney Meats. This was the biggest meat factory in the country and Crawford was their best buyer. He would go to cattle auctions all over the country and buy for Tunney. He could just look at a bull and know how much it weighed and what it was worth.

On our way there we stopped off at different auctions. Crawford would go in and 'Hey boy' would stay in the car. It was about 3pm in the middle of Belfast with lots of people around when Crawford said: 'Hey boy, pull over.' As I did, he kicked his door open and very swiftly got out of the car, suddenly looking much more agile than when we'd put him in. Then, to my utter horror, he squats down and just shits into his pants in front of God and nation, not to mention a load of girls coming out of school. I could not believe what I was seeing. This day was getting stranger and stranger.

'Hey boy, you go to the boot and get me some toilet paper.' I opened the boot and it was crammed full of toilet paper. It was at this point I knew I was in trouble. For the next six months I drove Crawford around and he shit himself each day, usually around four-ish – and I was the one who had to clean it up. 'Hey boy, pull over.' After a few days of this I figured how not to be in any cities at around four, made sure we were in the countryside close to a field with a gate. Most people would be embarrassed about just shitting like that, but not Crawford. Five miles later the stench would die down and we'd be heading for the next auction and the smell of cow shit.

Crawford had five kids, two girls and three boys. One girl lived with her brother up in Kildare at Crawford's farm. They dabbled in horses and drove BMWs and didn't visit Crawford very often. Jimmy, who was eighteen but looked about 30, lived with

Crawford, as did Brenda, who was about fifteen. There was another boy, Kevin, about seventeen, who lived in Kildare but visited often.

Jimmy and Kevin had a bit of an affliction. Jimmy looked like an albino: white, white hair and beef-coloured cheeks. He'd talk to himself as he walked. When I was running late in the morning Crawford would send Jimmy over the road to get me. My mother would hear him coming up the drive: 'Crawford gonna be mad, Crawford gonna be mad, Tommy in trouble, Tommy in trouble.' Then he'd mumble 'Tommy Byrne, Tommy Byrne', like if he didn't keep saying it he might forget where he's going. I'd walk behind him and he'd still be saying, 'Tommy Byrne, Crawford gonna be mad, Tommy in trouble.'

'Hey Jimmy. Shut the fuck up.'

'Oooh, I tell Crawford. Crawford gonna be mad.'

We walked up Crawford's driveway to the usual barrage of abuse. 'Hey boy bastard fuck shit.' Jimmy looked at me.

'Ooh, Crawford's mad.'

Sometimes Jimmy would come with us to the auctions. He knew quite a lot about them as he'd been going for years and the closer we got the more excited he'd become, and he'd go into auction mode: 'Who'll give me 375 for this fine bullock. 375, 375, come on yes, thank you sir. Three hundred and eighty-five, 385, 385, 385, 395, 400, 400, 410, 10, 10, 10, 420, 20, 20, 430, 30, 440, 40, 40, 40, 450, 50, 50, 50, 50, 460, 60, 60, 60, 470.' As the excitement rises, 'BANG. Four hundred and seventy and the bullock goes to Crawford Scott.'

Every now and then Jimmy's brother Kevin would

join us too. He knew nothing about selling cattle but a hell of a lot about football. It was only years later, when I saw the film *Rain Man*, that I figured out Jimmy and Kevin were autistic. So Kevin would commentate on imaginary games – also in the back of the car. 'George Best has the ball, down the centre to Charlton, passes it to Law who passes back to Best. George beats five defenders and shoots. It hits the crossbar. It rebounds back to Best and he nails it into the right corner of the net. GOAL! For Manchester United.'

'SOLD to Crawford Scott!' as Jimmy has just sold another bullock at the same time that Best has scored – in the back seat of a Peugeot doing about 110mph. Then: 'Hey boy, pull over.'

There were some compensations though. I would offer to service the Peugeot and so would take it home every weekend and change the oil, plugs and filters. Then I would syphon out the petrol and put it into my Formula Ford ready for Mondello Park and the next day's race. That Peugeot would get a service every weekend! And I did not feel one bit guilty. If I ever did, all I had to think of was, 'Hey boy, pull over.'

It was during this time that my girlfriend Caroline left to stay with her aunt in England because of her secret pregnancy. We'd been going out since we were about sixteen. She was the sister of my best friend, and also the best friend of my sister Cynthia. I'd known her for years before we started going out and had always looked on her as a pain in the arse. But one New Year's night at a pub in Blackrock where I was listening to a live band I bumped into Cynthia and Caroline. The band later played 'Sweet Caroline' and there was mistletoe everywhere and we kissed. Wow! She was no longer a pain in the arse, I decided. I was in love and I'd spend as much time as I could with her over the next few years. Then I got her pregnant.

PART TWO:

Up The Ladder

CHAPTER FIVE

Formula Ford

Four years after finally refusing to clean up Crawford's shitty pants one more time, Tommy Byrne prepared to climb aboard the F1 McLaren. The knacker from Dundalk, as a disapproving mother of a one-time girlfriend had labelled him, was now Tommy Byrne British Formula Ford Champion of 1980, British and European Formula Ford 2000 Champion of 1981, British Formula Three Champion of 1982 – and a pukka Grand Prix driver. He'd made his F1 debut earlier that year in a low-budget uncompetitive car called the Theodore. Now he was about to find out what it was like to drive a front-running F1 machine.

This test, awarded to the winner of the British F3 title in deference to Marlboro (which sponsored both the F3 championship and the McLaren F1 team) should have been the defining moment when a truly great F1 career – and the glittering awards and millions of dollars that brings – slotted into place. But it was doomed.

Regardless of how well Tommy performed in the subsequent few minutes – and he performed sensationally well – there was no way he was going to be helped by McLaren. For the reasons why, we need to understand the clash of cultures at work when Tommy Byrne met Ron Dennis, early in 1982.

There were just four years between Tommy's demeaning job of cleaning Crawford up and becoming an F1 driver on the brink of a McLaren deal – all with not a penny to his name. That says everything about Byrne's mercurial talent. Four years, when it was all happening for him, where a glorious future seemed to be opening out in front of him. With hindsight they were his golden years. But that short distance between those two very different worlds for sure played its part in his failure to hit it off with Dennis. Contrast the scenes he describes here with the world Ron Dennis inhabited by the time Tommy met him.

For all that I had to clean up his shite for six months, the job with Crawford did allow me to get over to England for the next stage of my career – not that he knew about that. I'd quit working for him about four months previously when I got a message that he wanted me back – I guess he'd had trouble finding anyone else willing to clean him up. It came at a time when we needed a tow car for the Formula Ford and he agreed to me putting a tow hook on the Peugeot if I came back.

One day he told me he wanted to go to Knock – which is a place where you go to get healed of ailments. We got there and walked around holding candles and at the end of the whole thing he gave the priests a cheque for £1,000 – which I wrote because of his shakes, and he just signed. He would hold the chequebook in one hand and the pen in the other but would hold the pen way up high, meaning he didn't have much of a grasp of it. His signature would start out OK but by the end he was so exhausted it just kind of petered out. This made it very easy to forge.

On the way home he looked at me and said, 'you know, I feel 100 per cent better.' Then I hit a hump-back bridge at about 80mph: 'aaargh, shit, fuck, bastard!'

After getting a taste for healing at Knock, he then decided to go to Lourdes in France. He was gone for about a week, giving me a great opportunity to use the car to visit England to talk to Vic Holman of PRS, the makers of the Formula Ford I'd been racing at Mondello. To pay for the trip I took one of Crawford's chequebooks, wrote myself a cheque for £1,500 and cashed it.

I'd built up quite a bunch of contacts from racing the PRS, plus I'd raced in the Formula Ford Festival in England the year before, entered by John Murphy, the owner of the racing school in Mondello where I'd started. Oh, plus my girlfriend Caroline was in London, having hid her pregnancy for months in Ireland from everyone but me. She went to London to stay with her aunt and have the baby. This was Catholic Ireland in the 1970s remember – she couldn't tell her parents, I couldn't tell mine. Apart from anything else, my fifteen-year-old sister had just got pregnant and was getting married the next year. Caroline ended up giving birth to a boy. I left Caroline soon afterwards and she put Jeff up for adoption. He finally got in touch with me years later.

I visited Bernard Devaney, the Irish driver who'd come to England to race with PRS, and he helped me with the introductions, to prepare for me coming over full-time in 1979. Although Bernard was having a lot of success in England, he was still very much in touch with the Irish racing community and it was him who talked PRS into hiring me. John McCambridge, an Irish car dealer based in London, was helping lay the groundwork for that move. John – who I'd been introduced to by Martin Donnelly Sr when I'd done the Formula Ford Festival – was to become my biggest supporter.

Anyway, with my business done, I headed back up to Stranraer to catch the ferry back to Dublin, ready to pick up Crawford the next day. He was looking good and I told him so. I said 'I bet you can get in the car yourself today.'

'You think so?'

'Sure.'

'OK, I'll give it a try.'

After a bit of shuffling he did it. But by the end of the journey home he was complaining about his back again. I eventually found out why he kept shitting himself. I came to collect him one morning and he was eating what looked like a bowl of cereal, except it wasn't: it was laxative! Not a spoonful, like you're supposed to take, but a bowlful. Hence the explosion at four every afternoon. Turned out that when he had a really good shite his back felt better!

After all the cleaning up I'd had to do, going into clothes shops to buy him new pants and stuff, it kind of pissed me off to find the uncontrolled bowel movements were of his own making. So when he started laughing at the idea of my becoming a professional, I was more than ready to walk. Naturally, he didn't pay me my last cheque, so I just wrote my own. I was out of there, on my way to London.

I was a 'professional' race driver, about to contest the 1979 British FF1600 Championship! Vic Holman, who ran PRS, was a customer of Lemsford Metal, which was run by a lovely guy called Roy Camp and his wife Lynn. Vic arranged that they be my personal sponsors. They became like a mother and father to me. Lynn would sit and listen to me and feed me – she even showed me how to fold a shirt. I also became very friendly with their son Martin and his wife Sue. The Camps were fantastic to me. I was welcomed into their home and treated as one of their own. Even when I later left PRS and was preparing and racing a Van Diemen, Martin and Sue would be there helping me. I could never begin to repay them.

John McCambridge was a bit of a lynchpin to the whole Irish car-dealing 'mafia' in London at the time. He called in lots of favours, and got me a lot of valuable help at this time too. He really laid the groundwork for my move.

'I was a fan,' recalls McCambridge. 'I'd been following racing since the 1950s and had a lot of contacts in it and in the car trade. I liked to see Irish guys doing well. When I'd met Tommy I'd been helping Martin Donnelly Sr run an Irish guy called Joey Greenan and Martin had introduced me to this little guy at the 1977 Formula Ford Festival. He was driving an old Royale and had never seen the place before. I noticed him out on the track at one point, controlling these huge slides, and he was not on the correct racing line, yet he did a 51.0s, which was a pretty quick time all things considered. We kept in touch and naturally I helped as much as I could when he came across full-time a couple of years later.'

John was an enormous help. I wouldn't have got as far as I did without him. He worked really hard on my behalf. He was there to pick me up from Gatwick when I finally made the move at the end of '78. He then proceeded to scare the living shit out of me by driving through London like a man possessed. We stopped off to see a lot of his car dealer friends along the way, and he'd embarrass me by telling them how good I was, and how far I was going to go. Then we'd be back in the car, heading off somewhere else at breakneck speed. He'd handbrake turn into parking spots, and he knew all the back alley shortcuts. Over the months, this became normal for me – this was just how he drove. One day, in London, he flew down the inside of an unmarked police car and I told him so. 'No, I did not,' he says. 'Yes, you did.' Next thing the lights come on and the policeman is stopping him. As the police car got alongside, John pulled over and stood full on the brakes, meaning the copper had to walk quite a way back to us. 'What sort of driving to you call that?' asks the policeman, 'have you any idea how fast you were going?' etc. John just said, 'If you're going to give me a ticket just get on and do it and stop with the lecture,' and the policeman would try to continue and John would just repeat, 'just write the ticket, will you and stop lecturing me,' and eventually you could see this young guy was getting flustered. He wrote out the ticket but was so frazzled that, as he walked back to his car, he left his hat on the roof of John's car. 'Hey, you left your hat!' John shouted, and the guy had to walk all the way back again. There was stuff like this virtually every time you got in a car with him.

Once, we were in Belfast and going through a

checkpoint. A British soldier came to the window, gun in hand, and John whispered to me, 'Don't give your Irish address.' I had no idea why, but I figured there must be a good reason, so I went along with it. The soldier asked for ID and we each gave him our driving licences and my licence had my Irish address on it. The soldier went away then came back and told us to pull over to the side and wait. We waited for over half an hour until an officer came to us and asked why I'd not given the address on my driving licence. I replied, 'Oh, I don't live there much anymore.' He then said, 'OK, you're free to go.' As we drove off I asked John what that was all about and why he didn't want me to give the Irish address. 'Fuck 'em,' he said, 'tell 'em nothing.' He came from the Falls Road and so hated the Brits and just wanted to fuck the soldiers about for the hell of it. That was John, but he would have done anything for me and I owe him and his lovely wife Derroca a lot.

John got me a job with one of his car dealer friends, Pat, and I'd be changing gearboxes, head gaskets and worked there for about three months. In the meantime I would meet up with my girlfriend Caroline whenever I could. She gave birth on 28 December 1978. In those days the father wasn't encouraged to be there at the birth, so I waited in a corridor outside, where I could hear everything. It wasn't nice. They went back to Caroline's auntie's house and I visited a few times. Once I had the baby and was throwing him over my shoulders when Caroline told me to stop as I might drop him. It was the final straw. I couldn't do it anymore. Complicating things further, I'd started seeing someone else, a girl called Angie. She was the daughter of Pat's girlfiriend. So I arranged to meet

Caroline one night in a pub, and I told her it was over, just like that. She cried and I felt bad, but it was done. I'm not proud of how I treated her – and our son – and later I realised I'd made a huge mistake. But it was too late.

I was soon living with Angie. She lived in these slum apartments near the garage. Her mother had an apartment downstairs, where she lived with Pat. I came to think of her mother as 'Panda' because her face was always black and blue from the beatings Pat gave her when he got a few drinks inside of him. He was a monster. One night Angie and I could hear him knocking seven colours of shite out of her mum, so Angie and I went down to try to stop it. We calmed him down and he sat down with Panda and apologised, and me and Angie went back upstairs. About ten minutes later we heard it all kick off again, so off I went again. This time it ended with him on top of me, choking me and taking a bite out of my cheek. I was begging for my life. He had the strength of ten men and was completely crazy. I came back upstairs. Angie used to rock back and forth when she was distraught. There we both sat rocking on the sofa together as Pat went another couple of rounds with Panda. After about fifteen minutes of this I was starting to get mad about the begging I'd had to do to save my ass and started looking for a weapon. There was a broken table in the flat from another of Pat's temper fits. I picked one of the legs from it and hid the others around the room and told Angie to call him upstairs and that when he came we'd beat the shit out of him. So she calls down the stairs, 'Leave my mum alone you Irish bastard. Come up here and I'll give you what you deserve.' So he comes running up the stairs and the first thing he does is punch Angie in the face, knocking her out cold. I grabbed my weapon and began hitting him across the skull with it. With the help of Panda I got him to the ground and every time he tried to get up I'd whack him again. I was hitting him so hard it was ricocheting up my arm. I actually began to feel sorry for him but I knew if I let him get up I was a dead man. I thought of running but decided to stay because he would have taken it out on the two women. Eventually he started to lick ass, 'Ah, Tommy, Angie. I'm sorry. I was only jokin' with yers. Let me up so I can have a fag.' I wasn't buying it but Panda was and the silly cow had been letting him get away with it for years. Suddenly a growl comes from him and he gathers his strength and goes to get up. I whacked him really hard: BANG, stay the fuck down, BANG, stay down – this time catching Panda's finger and breaking it. Eventually the police arrived and because he was such a mess they wanted to charge me, not him. But that was sorted when he threw another of his crazy fits in front of them. Now they believed me.

Half an hour later I was in the emergency room, lying in a bed getting a tetanus shot in my ass, with Pat in the next bed, getting fifty stitches in his head. He was talking and laughing about it all, friendly, like nothing had happened. The police assured me he would be spending about a week in jail. Angie, Panda and me went back to the flat. About 6am I was woken by the sound of breaking glass. The bastard was trying to get in through the front door. I grabbed a broom handle and began beating him back through the broken door window, shouting for Angie to call the police. He then took off, vowing he was going to get me. I believed him. There was only one door in that flat. There was a big back window and we were on the fifth floor. I know he was planning to throw me out of that window. The next day I was out of there. Not long after, Angie and I broke up.

Because of Pat's violence towards her mother Angie was on Valium – which I didn't know at the time. But it could make her a little crazy sometimes, especially if she mixed it with alcohol. This would sometimes surface when she was with me on a race weekend. She'd go completely nuts and here I was just about to get in the car. Vic Holman would appear and look at me with disgust, quite rightly. John McCambridge was also disgusted with me for putting a girl before my racing. It was best all-round when we split up.

So I've put the PRS on pole on my first visit to the Nürburgring, 14 miles long and supposed to be the place where you need years to learn. The PRS wasn't a great car but I'd won three races in it – races that it shouldn't have won. I was angry that this wasn't being realised. I was grateful to Vic and Steve Holman for giving me this drive – it was a massive deal for me – but I didn't have the time to waste; I needed to progress. It was that thing about respect again. I knew, coming from where I came from, that I had to win – and I wasn't. Well, not enough, anyway. Everyone's saying how I'm doing well, given that it was my first year and I had to learn all the tracks. Bollocks. I could learn any track within a few laps. They didn't think it possible that I could be as good as I was. To them, if a rookie was winning the odd race in it, it was a good car. It wasn't. It was uncompetitive, especially on the fast tracks like Thruxton and Snetterton, but these guys wouldn't listen to me. And that made me angry.

Occasionally it got the better of me, and the anger and desperation and the frustration of not being appreciated led me to dangerous driving. At the Nürburgring I had the pole at 9m 1.1s, three seconds faster than the next quickest guy. I told Vic Holman that here was the ultimate drivers' track – and that's why we were on pole, not because of his car. It made me angry when Peter Krober tried to pass me on the first lap, so I put him in the dirt flat out in fourth gear at the Pflanzgarten or something. I didn't care he broke his teeth – but the organisers did and they not only disqualified me from the win but wanted to lynch me.

Tommy didn't see out the 1979 season with PRS. He left to drive a Royale owned by David Winstanley, Tommy figuring it would be faster than the PRS. It wasn't. But Ralph Firman, boss of Van Diemen, the most successful of all the Formula Ford constructors, had been greatly relieved when Tommy had left PRS.

I quit PRS at the end of '79, just before the Festival, because they were not listening to me. They just couldn't accept that their car wasn't fast enough on the fast tracks and all I'd hear was how great a driver Van Diemen's Roberto Moreno was. In the end I could take no more of it. I knew I could take on Moreno – or anyone else for that matter – and come out on top, as long as I'd a level playing field. They just weren't getting it, didn't understand just what they had on their hands with me. So I left, even though it was a free ride, and I told them, 'Just you watch and you'll see who's quicker.' Fuckers.

Leaving PRS – the team that had given the raw penniless rookie his break with a fully paid-for drive, enabling him to become a professional racing driver – was a brave move, verging on foolhardy. With hindsight it just emphasises how much Tommy needed respect, how he absolutely could not tolerate anyone underrating how sensationally good he was. Knowing you're good is every bit as important in a top driver as being good: both qualities are necessary. Tommy had these qualities to an acute degree but – at the risk of being an amateur psychologist – you might wonder if the lack of respect so apparent in his upbringing meant he over-reacted to any perceived slight when applied to the one thing he knew he could do exceptionally well. On this occasion, the move had paid off. But it was a trait that would resurface later in his career, with less happy outcomes.

Actually, the timing of my leaving PRS was pretty dumb because that car was competitive on the short tracks, so would have been good at the Formula Ford Festival. Ralph told me later on that I was the one he'd been worrying about. It seemed like I'd impressed him and he was keen to get me onside for the following season rather than competing against him. He couldn't offer me a full works drive – they were reserved for the Brazilians Moreno and Raul Boesel, who were paying and had their own dedicated mechanics – but he made a car available for me and allowed me space in his workshop. Driving the Van Diemen I realised I'd been right to leave PRS – it was just a much faster car. In the PRS I'd never been able to take Russell bend at Snetterton flat out without lifting. In the Van Diemen I did it first time – it was easy. Same through the fast section around the back at Thruxton, flat out all the way – something that just hadn't been possible in the PRS.

Ralph and his wife Angie became like family. I rented a cottage from Angie near the factory and over the next three years I spent a lot of time with them. They'd have me round for Sunday lunch, I'd pick the kids up from school and Ralph was always the one I would go to for advice. I'd talk a lot with Angie, too. She seemed to like me – I guess both of us being Irish helped – and she was quite influential, in that she had Ralph's ear. The racing community being what it is, people read more into how well Angie and I got on than just the fact that she liked me. I liked her too – she's a nice person.

The little corner of Norfolk where Van Diemen was based was cut off from the rest of the world – farming country, great tracts of flat land speckled with a few small towns. In fact, about the only bit of land that wasn't flat was a big dip about 200 metres square in the middle of the Snetterton race-track called 'the bombhole', and that gives a clue how come there was even a racetrack there at all. The track was made from the perimeter roads of a wartime airfield, which had taken a hit from a German bomb. That track and the low cost of land had attracted the Lotus car company and its racing team in the 1960s, and from there a whole load of little motor racing specialist satellites had sprung up. Ralph's Van Diemen operation was one of these.

So there was a little racing community among a sleepy farming backwater, where nothing much had happened since that bomb hit the airbase 40 years earlier, and Ralph's little factory was where every wannabe world champion from around the globe wanted to get to – especially the Brazilians. About a dozen years earlier, Ralph had discovered Emerson Fittipaldi, the first Brazilian driver to make it into the big time and who went on to win a couple of world

*championships. Every rich young hot-shot in Brazil wanted
to follow in his footsteps, and it was a vein that Ralph mined
very well, founded his whole business on it really: took their
money, gave them fast cars and watched them win races in
the knowledge that they were paying him to advertise his
own cars, which everyone else would then buy. He was a
shrewd operator, though you might not have realised it on
first acquaintance.*

That's true – you might not, what with his Norfolk
twang and his funny toed-out eyes. Yeah, come over,
and if you're any good I'll do for you what I did for
Emerson. So he tended to get just the quick guys that
had already succeeded in Brazil, not the wankers.
And he tended also to get the quick guys with money,
usually family money, behind them. And that's the
background to how there was this whole aura bullshit
around the Brazilians in the UK at the time. They
seemed to get automatic respect without even having
to earn it. Raul Boesel was straight out of this mould –
from a rich family and very snobby with it. But
Roberto Moreno wasn't at all like that. He was about
the only Brazilian from a poor background that had
made it over to England, and he'd done it on his
talent alone.

He was good but I knew I was better – and after
hearing nothing from my team but how fantastic he
was, there was a lot of pressure on me at the first race
Moreno and me were paired in at Van Diemen – at
Brands Hatch, early 1980. It did not start off too well.
I tested at Snetterton two days before and was well
off the pace. I told Ralph it must be the engine, as it
certainly wasn't me, and to his credit he believed me.
He organised a new Auriga engine for the next day.

The day after that I went to Brands with no testing. Moreno, who'd tested, was on pole and I was second, but that was OK. The time difference was tiny and I was totally confident I'd beat him in the race. And that's what happened. I beat him off the line and he couldn't pass me for the rest of the race. That was all she wrote. So there, in the same car, I'd beat the Great Moreno in the Great Micky Galter-prepared Van Diemen. I was right: I am the best driver. Fuck all you unbelieving bastards, I showed you. It had been a year coming, because up until then only I knew how good I was, and now I was going to prove it. They'd created a monster by not believing in me, because I was so pissed off that I hadn't been given due respect. No one was going to stop me now. Just watch.

As you can no doubt sense, Tommy carried the anger in the car. But it was directed anger – he was hard and aggressive but usually this side of legal, his brain cool and collected, immense talent buying him all the time in the world to make the right calls every time. He had the perfect racing mentality in the car, a quality rare even among those who have the talent to drive very quickly. But even when things were going smoothly in the car, they rarely were off the track.

I was driving from London to Norfolk in one of John McCambridge's cars, an old VW bug with no tax or licence or any of the other legal requirements to drive. There was a police car in front of me on the motorway. I did not want to pass him, as he would see I was not legal, so I slowed down – and so did he. I slowed down some more – and so did he. Eventually, we were down to about 30mph. He pulled me over for going too slow on the motorway. Then he finds out that I have no tax, licence or insurance. Then things get worse because there is a spare set of number plates under the front seat with a spare battery and jump cables – all normal stuff for a car dealer to be carrying, but that fucker put two and two together and got fifty. There was an Irish terrorist on the run at the time and he was a master of disguises and that idiot somehow thought he had his man. Well, I was arrested and taken to the local nick. I guessed I would be there for a couple of hours and the guy would figure out pretty quick I was not a disguise artist, just a fucked up racing driver. So here I am sitting in the interrogation room and then it dawned on me that they were going to search my briefcase and it was at that moment I realised they would find two passports – and for sure that wasn't going to help matters.

About four months previously I had lost my Irish passport, and with a race coming up in Holland on the weekend. Because it took months to get an Irish passport, I had no option but to go to the post office and get a British visitor's passport. The only problem being I'm not British. I told a white lie and said I was born in Newry, County Down, instead of Dundalk, County Louth. Everything went great. I went to Europe, won the race, and forgot about it until I was driving down the road in my race truck and lo and behold, my Irish passport falls down from behind the dash: so I threw it in my briefcase with my false passport. Not one of my best ideas.

Sure enough, in comes your man and now he really thinks he is going to get a promotion. He says to me, 'Now, Tommy, is there anything else you have to tell us?' and I said, ' No.' I'd guessed he found the two passports but decided to bluff it out, just in case he hadn't. He left and came back and told me to relax, that there were a couple of fellows coming from London to talk to me and it would be a while. About four hours later, two detectives walked into the room with my two passports in their hands. They invited me to explain, so I told them about the race in Holland and how I found the other passport. It was all cleared up in about ten minutes. Of course, your uniformed cop did not get any promotion, but he did charge me with passport fraud and I had to go to court a month later. More probation, more fines.

Another time I was stopped by a policeman, I decided I'd treat it like John McCambridge did and just be really aggressive – it always seemed to work for John. I'd gone round a roundabout a bit fast and the copper asks what sort of driving did I think that was and I said, just like John: 'Stop with the lecture. Just give me a ticket if you're going to and if not, stop wasting my time.' Well the guy made me take a breathalyser. I'd not had a drink but he said the result wasn't clear and he was taking me to the station. He had me thrown into a cell, kept me there about two hours, then let me go, saying I'd passed the breathalyser after all. The moral of the story was you can get away with being aggressive if you're six foot five, like John was, but not when you're five foot five.

One of Tommy's team-mates in the Van Diemen Formula Ford team, Raul Boesel, came from a background more typical for a would-be F1 driver. At his family home in Brazil he'd had servants. Now he was living in a rented house near Snetterton and spending time with people below his social station.

You could see that Boesel looked down on Moreno. We were testing at Snetterton one day and a bunch of us were standing at the pitlane barrier, watching someone come through the daunting Russell bend, which in those days was flat out in an FF1600 and where a lot of drivers were injured over the years. Moreno decided he needed to piss and so he just took that great monster out of his trousers and pissed right over the Armco, then he wound it up and put it away. We were all laughing – but not Boesel, who gave him a look of complete disdain. He gave me that look once when I took the fucker swimming in Thetford. He didn't speak English too well and I'd been the nice guy, keeping him company and taking him around. So we're at these baths and he's just about to dive into the pool and I shout, 'Raul, sssssstooooop! You have your watch on!' He gave me that same look he'd given Moreno before explaining, very condescendingly, that it was an expensive waterproof watch, like I was some sort of peasant who'd never heard of such things. Oh, silly me.

I hit it off much better with Moreno. Ralph had the three of us concentrating on different championships. I focused on the P&O series, Moreno on the TT and Boesel on the RAC. But whenever Moreno did a round of 'my' championship or I did a round of 'his' championship, we would help each other, try to let the other go free while acting as tail gunner and keeping the rest behind.

By halfway through the season I was leading two of the British championships and there was a free weekend, so I talked Ralph into entering me in a race at Mondello. It would be fun to go back there, I thought. I'd no concern about taking on the locals.

They were a bunch of nobodies, I thought, and I'd have no trouble beating them. How wrong I was! I didn't even get pole position – this new guy, John McCracken, took it. I'd never even heard of him, this guy from dirty Dublin. It was the talk of the pitlane – Tommy Byrne's finished, there's a big new star now. Well, I'll just get him at the start, I thought to myself, do my trademark short-brake, get him all crossed up, then disappear into the distance. No problem. But there WAS a problem – he beat ME off the line. Then proceeded to block me for twenty laps. Going into the last lap it was obvious I wasn't going to get round him – and this was serious. If he beat me, not only wouldn't I be the fastest guy in Formula Ford any more, I wouldn't even be the fastest Irish guy! So going into the hairpin for the last time I decided if I wasn't going to win it, neither was he. As he was turning in I took to the grass and T-boned him, taking both of us out. As you can imagine, McCracken was looking to kick my arse after the race but I had my Dundalk contingent with me and last time I saw McCracken my uncle John had him by the throat.

I bumped into him again ten years later. He was in a bar in Chicago with Bernard Devaney, who introduced us. Turned out he was a bad ass and had had to leave Ireland for reasons unknown. He was a crazy bastard! Later that night three guys in the bar began to fuck with him. He smashed a bottle across the bar and attacked them and all three ran out of there. At this moment I got a flashback to that time at Mondello and thanked my lucky stars he hadn't caught up with me that day! We later became good friends and laughed about that day in Mondello. I was just getting to know him well when he was killed in a car crash. It was no surprise to anyone who knew him – he was totally crazy on the road. But beneath it all he was a lovely guy who'd do anything for you – so long as he was on your side.

Anyway, I got waylaid there again, didn't I? Back to my 1980 Formula Ford season. Much as I didn't care for my team-mate Boesel, the tension wasn't really between the drivers. The fact that I was winning more than either of the Brazilians – I was keeping a pretty close tally on it – despite doing all the work on the car myself, created a problem with Moreno's mechanic, Mickey Galter. Mickey lived in that shop and worked on that car day and night. It was by far the cleanest, best-prepared car around and Mickey was justifiably very proud of his work. Whenever Moreno won, Mickey would go around gloating. He'd be ecstatic and would let you know that Moreno had won because of Mickey's car. He would hang his laurel on the wall every Monday morning and spend the next hour or so strutting through the factory chatting with all the other mechanics who built the cars. This was his life; he lived to win races. But as with every special mechanic he had his problems. He could be a psycho and would lose his temper with spanner-throwing fits – and God help poor Moreno when he lost.

At first Mickey helped me some. And any success I had, I would tell Mickey that I appreciated his part in it. But he didn't like it when I started winning more races than Moreno. For sure, I used to wind him up about it too, pointing it out maybe a bit too much. But I wasn't going to listen to him all day telling me how they were going to win all these races. Plus, I'd turn up at the workshop at ten or eleven, when he had to be there at eight, being an employee. So I'd waltz in there, all cocky, while he'd been hard at work for an hour or two. Then, often as not, at the weekend I'd win.

Well, one Monday morning I walked in, having just won a race on Sunday. I see there's a newspaper lying on top of the gearbox of my car. Jokingly, I asked who's it was and when Mickey said it was his I said, 'Well get it to fuck off my race car,' just in the way of banter. So he walks over, but instead of taking the newspaper, he punches me around the back of the head.

I couldn't believe what was happening. This bastard was hitting me. I went nuts. I looked around for a weapon, found a roll bar and whacked him on the shoulder with it. We were running around this car, screaming and shouting at each other – and all the others are just standing by. He caught me and started beating me in the head again and still no one stopped him. Then the fight moved into Ralph's office and it was Ralph who broke us up. I went to Angie's office to calm down. I just could not believe that this guy could just beat me up at work and Ralph thought it was no big deal. If it had been Boesel or Moreno getting beat up I knew it would have been a very different story. Here I was, leading two championships for the team, and they're not even bothered that one of their mechanics beats me up. I was nearly crying with temper. It nearly flared up again when I went outside and Galter was there bragging to the others about how he beat me up, sneering at me. I went at him with a shovel but someone took it off me before I got to him.

I went home to the cottage I was sharing with my friend Dave Meehan, a mechanic at the team, and just to cap a perfect day I was up on the kitchen roof adjusting the TV aerial when it caved in and I fell through it. I just lay there on the ground and couldn't stop myself crying.

I believe Ralph enjoyed the whole thing – and I base that belief on what happened a year later when we were over at Mondello. Galter prepared the car of another Irish driver, Martin Donnelly Jr. His father, Martin Snr, was in the bar, telling anyone who would listen how his son's car was a piece of shite and that's why he was struggling. He was shitfaced, as he often was. As he went to the toilet he could hardly walk. Galter went in after him and next thing you know Martin Snr is laying in a pool of blood in the bathroom. Now I'm not saying that Ralph – who just sat there with his whiskey looking pleased with himself throughout – told Mickey to do it, but he knew Mickey and it wouldn't surprise me if he'd put the idea in his head. To this day Galter probably doesn't realise how lucky he was. An English bully in Ireland beating up an old, drunk, and very popular Irish guy: he was very lucky not to have been shot. Really.

Tommy won the 1980 P&O and RAC FF1600 titles, with a total of eleven wins – two more than Moreno, four more than Boesel – from 22 starts. The P&O had been assigned as 'his' championship by Van Diemen, in that there would be no competition from Moreno and Boesel. The RAC was supposed to be Boesel's but when he failed to finish the first round and Byrne won, all bets were off. Tommy clinched the title in the final round at Snetterton in October by leading Moreno and Boesel across the line for a Van Diemen 1-2-3. The next year, while Tommy was dominating in the next category up, FF2000, Ayrton Senna was blitzing the FF1600 scene.

Although Senna's 1981 FF1600 season is correctly recalled as one of dominance, he took only one more victory than Byrne had in 1980 – and from more starts and with arguably lesser opposition. And Senna had no need to be preparing his own car.

CHAPTER SIX

Ayrton Senna

There were lots of things Tommy Byrne didn't know. He didn't know tomorrow had a limit, that he wasn't just going to keep on surfing this beautiful wave forever, blessed by a gift bestowed on him from who-knows-where, following a serene path through the white waters of a savage sport. Falling off was what other people did. It had nothing to do with him. So he thought. He also didn't know what on earth Ayrton Senna was talking about in early 1982 when he burst into the Van Diemen office, ranting and raving, calling Tommy 'a fucking thief'.

'What the fuck yer talking about?' says Tommy, bewildered.

'You stole my fuckin' wheels.'

'What fuckin' wheels?'

'The wheels of my Alfasud, you bastard.'

'Don't call me a bastard, you bastard.'

There was a scuffle and Angie Firman broke us up. He left shouting abuse, me shouting it back. It was just the latest in a series of niggles with Senna da Silva as he called himself then.

It had started at the end of 1980, when Ralph had promoted me to his works FF2000 car, in the next formula on the racing ladder to F1. My sponsor, John McCambridge, was a car dealer and whenever anyone needed cars I'd get them through John. Ralph told me he'd got this Brazilian coming over for '81 and that he needed a car, could I organise it? So I sorted out an Alfasud through John and drove it up to Ralph's. Ralph's already calling this Brazilian 'fast man' before he's even arrived. Here we go again, I thought. One of Ralph's old drivers, Chico Serra, has been telling him about this 'fast man' in Brazil for years and now he was finally coming over. I was sick of hearing it, to be honest. 'Fast man' – and he's not even in the country yet!

Ralph replaced me in his 1600 team with a couple of guys who didn't get the job done. But Ralph also had 'fast man' – the rich, pain-in-the arse Senna da Silva, who was even more arrogant than me. But he was paying for his drive. He was paying because Ralph knew he had money. That's how it works. If you're very quick, but a knacker from Dundalk, you might get a chance if someone like Ralph sees you as a way of enhancing the worth of his business. If you're very quick but from a rich Brazilian family, already a millionaire, you will have to pay for the chance because someone like Ralph knows that someone like Senna will place a value on what Ralph can offer his career prospects. Part of what made that drive so attractive to Senna would have been what I'd done with it the previous year.

Anyway, I wipe up again in Ford 2000 just as Senna is doing in Ford 1600. We both spend time around the Firmans but he doesn't mix socially with the other drivers around Snetterton. It's soon pretty obvious that he resents the fact he's paying for his ride, whereas I'm getting paid for mine. He talks to Angie and Angie talks to me and I get to hear his gripes. 'Tommy does this wrong, Tommy does that wrong, it's not fair that Tommy gets paid when I have to pay,' etc, etc. Angie replies, 'Well, Tommy can't be doing that much wrong, he's winning races and championships.'

So it's coming up to the time, at the end of the season, for the Formula Ford Festival, which is like the world championship of Ford 1600. And suddenly Senna decides he's going to retire and move back to Brazil, saying something about how he's disenchanted with a sport that asks the driver to pay money. And so Ralph needs his car to win the Festival. His business for the next year pretty much depends upon it, but now his hot-shot's gone home in a flounce. 'Tommy, will you come back to 1600 and win the Festival for me?' Of course.

So I test Senna's car and it's not that great, I gotta tell you. I'm not convinced. And maybe Ralph's not either, because the next day he collars me, saying: 'I've got Ayrton waiting at the airport in Brazil ready to come back for the Festival if I really want him to. Are you really sure you can win the race?' Ayrton at the fuckin' airport, like he can do the job that I can't! Fuck off! 'Hell yes, no problem,' I say.

I start the first heat from pole position, but jump the start and after a couple of laps I see the 10s penalty from the officials; so I have to win by over 10s. Which I do by less than a second. The quarter-final I win pretty easily. The first semi I realise I'm in trouble: Rick Morris in the works Royale is up my ass for all twelve laps, and I'm not running the times that I should be. I shit myself: could I lose the Festival? I start complaining to Dave Meehan, my mechanic. I don't know what's wrong with it, I just know there's something, as it's certainly not the driver. We put new shocks on for the final and I start from pole. But in the race Morris is all over me again, like shite on a shovel. It's a long fifteen laps. I try everything to shake him. I try throwing the car around, I try being smooth, but every time I look in the mirror, there he is, about 1 foot away. But with two laps to go, he makes a mistake at Paddock Bend and drops a couple of car lengths. Now I know I have the festival won, in Senna's car, just like I promised Ralph. It was not quite as easy as I expected, but I did it.

While Senna was in Brazil, 'retired', the Alfasud – which he was supposed to pay Ralph for but never did – just stood around in the Van Diemen car park. Ralph had another Brazilian, Mauricio Gugelmin, coming over for '82 and was going to sell the car to him. I had an Alfasud too and I was always getting punctures in it. But instead of getting it fixed, I'd just go and borrow a wheel from the other one. I thought nothing more of it.

Suddenly, Senna 'unretires' and comes back to continue his career in '82 – in Ford 2000, while I move up to F3. I was just happy I'd won the Festival – for Ralph and myself. Winning that race opened up opportunities for me. I guess Ayrton wasn't quite as happy about it all as I was.

It's actually doubtful that Senna ever had any real intention of retiring. Much more likely, he just figured that the Festival was a bit of a lottery – you can be taken out in a heat or a semi through no fault of your own but no one remembers that, only who won. He'd dominated the category all year and now he was about to risk that reputation in a lottery. So he stepped down. Then, when the problem had passed, he reappeared and continued on his path.

If you subscribe to this theory – and it certainly stacks up, tallies with the ruthless way Senna operated – then you'll see it's little wonder Senna called Byrne a thief. Not only did Tommy's winning the Festival in Ayrton's actual car rather sully Senna's plan to quietly step down, it also led directly to Tommy getting an F3 race – for a team that Senna had been in discussions with for 1982, interrupting those plans too! All caused by an initial opportunity Ayrton himself had inadvertently given him! From Ayrton's emotion-skewed perspective, Tommy stole his Festival drive, stole his F3 opportunity, and now, just to top it all, he's discovered he's stolen the wheels of his road car too! Mix in some Latin red mist and it's easy to understand the furious, flustered Ayrton and his shouts of 'fucking thief'.

So, while it probably hurt Senna that Tommy won the Festival in his car, the real point is that Senna's money had given him the choice to dictate his own path as he saw fit. It worked out on this occasion that the choice his money gave him accidentally benefited Tommy instead, but that wasn't really the point – not long term, anyway.

I've no idea what Ayrton's real motives were. I just grabbed an opportunity as it was thrown in front of me. I had no plan. I had no money to make a plan. Just taking what was put in front of me had worked this time – it led to my driving for free in F3 the following year – but over a career how many times would it? If you're not steering your own destiny, how do you stay on top of the wave? These are hindsight thoughts. At the time I was enjoying that wave so much. I was cock of the walk. Money? I was totally certain the millions were just down the line. That's why I wasn't even too bothered when I didn't have my own place to stay in, when I was just copping a couch for a night here and there.

Yeah, I guess the wheels were just the final straw for Ayrton. Why else would he go nuts over a couple of borrowed wheels from a car that wasn't even his? I guess when he was calling me a 'fuckin' thief' he was really talking about me winning the Festival in his car and getting to F3 because of it, not about the wheels. Did I feel bad about that? Fuck off did I! He'd got a million head starts on me already, all with dollar signs beside them. I'd just sneaked a few back.

The Ford 2000 season was done on an absolute shoestring. Ralph needed someone quick in his 2000 car, as he hadn't really established Van Diemen there. But he had no proper budget for it. He wanted me to prepare the car myself again to save money, but I felt I'd done enough to deserve not to have to do that anymore. Finally he relented and agreed to run me, but it was all very last-minute and I hadn't even tried the car before the first race, at Brands, and we had a lot of problems in qualifying, putting me halfway down the grid. The two Ford 1600 mechanics came and gave me some grief as I was sitting on the grid, asking me what I was doing all the way down there. I told them not to worry, just to watch where I was by the first corner and that I'd give them a wave.

At the green Tommy took off like a rocket, opting for the long but clear way round the outside of the pack into Paddock Bend. Braking outrageously late, he passed car after car around the outside and was up to third place. As he was applying the opposite lock in the wildly sliding car, he remem-bered he'd promised to wave. So he took his right hand from the wheel and gave them one. It was a George Best moment. Cocky? Oh yes, but a beautiful illustration of how racing a car on the absolute edge took so little of Tommy's mental capacity. That was about the last time that season that he was beaten as he dominated both the European and British FF2000 championships, winning thirteen races.

Although I won a lot of races and both the titles, I recall that season as a real shit-fight, in that we really didn't have the running budget to do it properly, we had a fairly poor engine and Ralph was constantly on at me, telling me unless I found some money he was going to pull the plug. I responded the only way I could by winning the races. With me leading both the British and European championships, I knew he would find it very difficult to just pull out. But after one race at Oulton Park I think he really meant it. I'd been leading the race but Dave Coyne in the Delta was on my ass giving me a hard time. I was hugging the grass on the right so there was no way he was going down the inside and he was so close behind I could see the balls of his eyes. That's when, halfway down the straight I brake-tested him, to let him know he couldn't mess with me. I didn't respect him as a driver at that time. I just thought the Delta must be good or have a good engine. It later turned out that he was a great driver. We both crashed out and Ralph went ballistic afterwards, saying why was he even bothering if I couldn't finish – and I hadn't even told him I'd done it deliberately! He was so pissed off he got in the car and drove home, leaving me to find my own way back to Snetterton. But by the next race we were back on speaking terms.

After clinching the titles as recounted, Tommy then stood in for Ayrton Senna in the category below, FF1600, and won the Festival. The prize for which was an F3 drive with Murray Taylor Racing in the season-ending F3 race at Thruxton. There he made a sensational debut in the category. In his first qualifying session he was under the existing lap record. He eventually qualified and raced second to Dave Scott, an established front runner who'd been doing the series all year. He then took in one final FF2000 race at Brands Hatch – and blitzed it.

I was pissed off I didn't win the F3 race actually. On the second lap I ran wide at the Complex and took a big chunk out of the undertray, which gave me too much understeer for the rest of the race. But for that, I'm sure I'd have won.

Tommy was making good on his self-assessment of being a truly great racing driver. Anyone able to run this sequence of success in three different major career ladder categories against top international opposition – there were just three weeks covering the Festival win, the debut F3 podium and the final FF2000 victory – with the pressure to shine absolute, in that his career would likely have come to a full stop if he hadn't, was a very special talent indeed. No one before or since has come close to emulating the feat.

Murray Taylor recalls how fate brought Tommy and him together. 'I was running Raul Boesel in F3 in '81. He had some talent and some money so was a good combination. But the guy I really was keeping an eye on for '82 was Ayrton Senna. It seemed obvious he was the hotshot – and he spent quite a bit of time that year in our garage, as he was quite friendly with Boesel. So I did a pitch to Marlboro, who, as well as sponsoring the F3 championship, also backed the FF1600 Festival. I said that we would run the winner of the Festival in the non-championship F3 race at Thruxton, fully expecting that to be Senna. As it happened, it ended up being Tommy. I'm sure Ayrton was a bit pissed off about that. But Tommy did a stunning job for us at Thruxton and I couldn't help but be enormously impressed.

'But still I was planning on getting Senna for '82. He was clearly a fantastic driver and he seemed to have access to a budget. We'd got quite far down discussing it and then suddenly he'd apparently gone home and retired. He didn't return my calls over the winter and so I set about trying to pull something together with Tommy. I got sponsorship on a race by race basis with Tommy as the driver. We had to win just to get to the next race and Tommy just kept winning. We scraped together Shell, Lucas and a few other bits and pieces. It was the toughest year I ever did but also the most rewarding.'

It's impossible to know what was going on behind the scenes with Senna, now that he's no longer here to tell us. But let's thread together what we do know. He had been in discussion with Taylor about an F3 drive for '82 at a time when it looked as if Tommy wasn't going to be in F3 through lack of finance. Dennis Rushen was running the Van Diemen FF2000 team for '82 and had approached Senna in late '81 about the idea of him being the '82 FF2000 driver, but that he would need to bring a budget of £15,000. Senna thanked Rushen for his interest but declined, telling him that he'd be doing F3 in '82. Rushen went ahead and made other plans and so was surprised when, in early '82, Senna got *back in touch about the FF2000 drive. Rushen explained that he was already committed to running someone else and to run a second car he'd need to bring more than the originally quoted £15,000. At which point Senna got very angry, demanding that Rushen honour his original offer. Eventually Senna got Ralph Firman involved and somehow a deal was massaged through, whereby Rushen ran Senna in FF2000 in '82. If you buy into the theory that Senna deliberately missed the Festival to keep his reputation for dominance intact, you might also ponder that he reckoned he couldn't dominate British F3 if Tommy was contesting it – and so therefore switched to FF2000, where he could continue to dominate, leaving him ready to progress to dominating F3 in '83, when Tommy (presumably) would have moved on. It seems odd that Senna, son of a very rich man, with access to any number of wealthy backers from Brazil, should have suddenly been struggling for budget. Was Senna actually reluctant to go head-to-head with Tommy? It would certainly further explain his apparently over-the-top anger towards Tommy about those missing Alfasud wheels.*

In 1982 Senna duly succeeded Tommy as British and European FF2000 champion, just as he had succeeded him as British FF1600 champion the year before and just as he would succeed him as British F3 champion in '83. They were the outstanding two drivers of the junior categories, no one else had a look-in and, pragmatically, it made good sense they didn't take each other on at this early stage. If Senna was avoiding Tommy, you couldn't fault his logic.

CHAPTER SEVEN

I'm The Man, Me And Stan

I'd won the first two races of my Formula Three season, driving for a Kiwi called Murray Taylor. He was a good guy but he had no cash to run me. He just said: 'You keep winning and I'll keep finding the money.' So I'd done my part of the bargain and Murray had arranged that I go and see Ron Dennis, boss of the McLaren F1 team. Murray had spoken to him, with the idea that if I signed a McLaren contract giving Dennis first option on my future services, McLaren would fund the rest of my F3 season. Now Dennis wanted to meet me before making a decision.

So off I went to Woking. I was shown into a room and there was Dennis, his partner Teddy Mayer and Tyler Alexander, one of the directors of the team. Ron did most of the talking, then started asking questions. I'm an open sort of guy and just answered very honestly.

'Where were you born?' Dundalk. 'What was your education?' None. I left school at fifteen and got a job. 'What does your father do?' Works in a factory making shoes. 'How many brothers and sisters do you have?' Four sisters and a brother. 'How good are you as a driver?' The best in the world.

Then I popped in the question of getting money to finish the F3 season. 'All our money is tied up in R&D,' he replied.

'What's R&D?' I asked quizzically.

You could have heard a pin drop. I knew I'd just made a bad mistake. He looked at me like I was The Knacker from Dundalk and in a tone you wouldn't use on a dog, he sneered, 'research and development'.

If I'd had a shovel I'd have dug a hole and jumped into it. I was the absolute opposite of what he was looking for, regardless of how fucking good I was. He wanted someone shiny and educated, someone at ease in his world and that of his backers, someone who wouldn't make them feel uncomfortable I guess. Going there on my own had been a huge mistake. Twenty-five years later, I still feel that moment. It fucking haunts me.

A pre-contract giving Dennis an option on Byrne's services was later signed. But as no money was ever exchanged, it wasn't binding. Murray Taylor's got a take on the complex dynamic between Dennis and Byrne.

'To understand Tommy you have to go to Dundalk. That's what he's about. Came from a very poor family, a streetwise little guy. I think he didn't make it because his face didn't fit. If he'd come along now, where you have manufacturers picking up the talent as it comes through, he would've made it on merit. When he came through it was all about rich kids

and Brazilians with company sponsors. He was not a groomed corporate animal. I'm very fond of him, he has the greatest character and an enormous natural talent.

'If you're looking at the one thing that probably defined his F1 career as limited it was his relationship with Ron Dennis. Tommy was a little rat bag sometimes. We had no control over him. He was very gifted but always on the back foot, looking for money, sleeping on people's floors. I think maybe what Ron saw was something he'd spent the last ten years getting away from. He'd come from the backstreets, pulled himself up by his bootstraps and there was maybe a bit of recognition of that.

'I had some sponsor meetings in Ireland. One guy was very interested, the guy was nibbling and Tommy made some inappropriate remark thinking it was a done deal. You saw the guy thinking 'hang on'. Tommy didn't have the sophistication to make it in the plastic world of racing. He was his own man, a little leprechaun.

'Tommy could drive you nuts and he could be very kind. People saw him as simple but there was actually quite a depth there.'

A knacker from Dundalk wasn't a profile the pinnacle of the sport could easily accommodate, just as it had earlier had problems accommodating a Brummie called Nigel Mansell, despite frequent demonstrations of his talent. No, it much preferred exotic wealthy South Americans with the easy charm that a monied upbringing brings. Tommy's the sport's defining case study though. He is what he is, a force of nature, a victim of nurture. He was a phenomenal talent in the car, a magical mix of neurons accidentally brought together, all motivated by ambition born of desperation to escape the world he'd been born into. He had the arrogance and self-belief of the sublimely gifted but was not equipped to deal with the fall-out of that or the injustices of what remains a very elitist sport.

Interestingly, a year or so after Tommy's interview at McLaren, Ron Dennis sat Ayrton Senna down in the very same office – and made him the offer that Tommy had sought, to fund the F3 season in exchange for first option on his future services. Senna, as well as being comparably devastating in the car to Byrne, was much more the sort of persona Dennis was looking for, and at the time of Ron's meeting with Tommy, Senna was already creating a big impact on the junior racing scene. Had he not been, had there not been someone of a similar stature to Tommy just a year behind, then Byrne's talent might have been irresistible to Dennis, regardless of the social stigma of his background.

Senna turned Dennis down. But then Senna, with his backers, was able to fund his own F3 season. And Senna never had to work for anyone like Crawford. Tommy and Ayrton were from very different worlds. One of those worlds the ambitious Dennis never wanted to see again, the other he aspired to.

But did Tommy really blow his chances with Dennis right from that first meeting? Ron says not. 'No, he had a certain personality but that didn't sway my judgement. I would have been happy if he'd fulfilled his potential in a McLaren. There was just nothing suitable within the team for him at that time.'

After making a good impression in my F3 prize drive, Murray Taylor got enthusiastic about the idea of running me in the '82 championship. Particularly as the guy he'd been intending to run, Ayrton Senna, had suddenly gone cold on him.

Problem was, Murray had no money either. All he had was the team and the '81 car, which he'd had updated to the new spec. He'd no money to run it. But he put an entry in for the first race – at Silverstone early in March. He told me I had to win – otherwise we wouldn't have the money to do the next race. I wasn't too worried. I tested the car, it felt pretty good and there was no one on that grid I knew I couldn't beat. So the flag drops, I quickly pass the two guys that had qualified ahead of me, and won pretty comfortably. Murray had got some trade backers and bits and pieces and the win brought some more money in and enabled us to do Thruxton a week later. There, it was the same deal: 'You've got to win, Tommy.' So I did. I put it on pole and led from start to finish. The others didn't even see which way I'd gone.

It was between this race and the next one that I had my disastrous meeting with Ron Dennis. So I was desperate to do well – to show Dennis that I wasn't just winning but wiping the floor with everyone, hoping this would make amends for the bad impression I'd obviously made with him. That was the frame of mind I was in – and it was a disaster. I'd already won four championships in two years and here I was on my way to a fifth, yet I still felt I wasn't getting the respect I deserved and everyone was still raving about the Brazilians – whether that be Moreno or Senna. I felt that to get to F1 I had to look sensational, and that winning simply wasn't enough.

The race was wet and I just took off. I couldn't even see anyone in my mirrors by the end of the first lap. I was killing them. Then I spun at the chicane. By the time I got restarted I was halfway down the field. I got back up to about fourth, but in my anger I was trying too hard and spun again. I couldn't believe it. I'd lost the fuckin' plot at a crucial time. I'd never done that in a racing car before. Murray and the mechanics were very pissed off afterwards – but not half as pissed off as me. It taught me a lesson: winning was all that was needed. It didn't matter by how much. After that I won the next three races in a row. But my feeling was that Dennis had stopped watching by then – if he ever had been.

By this time John McCambridge had started bringing his friend Stan – another car dealer from London – to my races. Stan began to get into it in a big way, bringing along his friends. They began hiring circuits and having their own little race series with their own road cars, giving each other trophies for the best accidents. Stan loved being around the racing scene and became my minder: he'd be by my side, carrying my helmet and gear, generally being there and giving me support. He was there at the Las Vegas Grand Prix when I walked through the lobby of the hotel in my racing suit. I hated seeing racing drivers posing in their race suits, and here I was doing the same – because the paddock was just outside the hotel. But that didn't stop me from being embarrassed as everyone looked.

Stan and I went to the best restaurants, drank the best wine and he would always pay. He was the life and soul of the party and would always be dressed in expensive designer gear and wearing expensive jewellery and the mandatory Rolex. He was great fun to be with.

It was Helen, Stan's girlfriend, who talked me into getting my teeth fixed. I didn't like dentists much and the last memory I had of them was when I had four teeth pulled in one day. Even worse than the pain was the mental torture of sitting in the waiting room listening to the screams of the kids ahead of me and knowing it was going to be my turn next. But Helen told me that I could be put asleep and she organised the whole thing for me. She dropped me off at their dentist; I was in there for hours as I was getting a whole new front row of teeth. When it was all done and I woke up I looked in the mirror and I really didn't know what to think, as now I had teeth and before I did not. Helen's sister Lindy, who I was dating at the time, came to pick me up. I got into the car all groggy. ' OK, show them to me,' and I smiled. 'Oh my God they are beautiful Tommy, I love them.' Then Helen told me the same thing as did everybody who saw them except Angie Firman, who said, 'Oh my God Tommy, can you get your old ones back? I hate them.'

Lindy and I broke up and I met her a few years later and we got to talking about all the fun we had together and she told me, 'You know, Tommy, I really loved you, I even lied about your teeth. When I seen them that first time I nearly shit myself because they looked like fuckin' tombstones.'

Helen and Stan taught me about the finer things in life – designer clothes, fine foods, etc. I worked with Helen selling cushion covers in the East End of London to make the money for my tombstones.

Stan was a great friend back when I was The Man on the track. Then, he was The Man off the track. But I saw one night how you wouldn't want him to be your enemy. He took me to this club and the bouncer wouldn't let us in for some reason. So we walked back to Stan's car – a brand-new BMW – and waited. We waited there until the club closed and the bouncer walked out to get in his car. At this point Stan started the engine, switched on the headlights and rammed this guy's car about three times, totally trashing both cars.

He had some dodgy friends too. We went to this Italian restaurant once, where a load of Italians joined us, very obviously mobster types. One of them had brought his girlfriend. Anyway, my meal arrived and I did my usual and just got tucked straight in. Suddenly this mobster starts screaming at me: 'Have some respect! Wait for the lady to start, then you can start.' I hated being told what to do. Especially back then. When you're a racing driver, the big star, nobody ever tells you anything negative, and you get away with a lot of shit you shouldn't. So I was wanting to say: 'You talking to me? You fuckin' fat criminal with your fat whore – respect this.' Then give him the finger and walk out. But I had just enough sense to know that I might not see tomorrow if I tried that. It took some doing, but I swallowed my pride rather than my food – and stayed quiet.

Stan would have a motorhome at the circuit and I often used to stay in it. A bunch of us were in it one night at Silverstone. I was in the bit above the cab, together with Calvin Fish, a friend who was racing in FF2000 at the time against Senna. Every time we turned around, the bottom of the bunk would hit the roof of the cab and it sounded like it was doing a lot of damage. We were too drunk to care at the time but in the morning I got out to have a look at the cab and was amazed to find there was no damage. I thought no more of it, because I had a race to worry about.

Actually, there was something to worry about. This was the race where my winning sequence stopped. Murray had hired another driver, Tim Lee Davey I think it was, and Murray gave him my car and updated one for me. Immediately, I went from domination to struggling to stay in the top six. I knew straight away what had happened. The new updated car was the problem. Well it took me six races and a lot of fighting with my engineer to convince them that it was not me. Good drivers just do not lose their talent overnight.

The next race was going to be the British Grand Prix support event at Brands Hatch – and no way was I going to look like a tosser in front of the F1 teams: so I quit. I told Murray that if he wasn't prepared to get a new chassis, I wasn't going to drive for him any more – even though we were leading the championship. Murray was in tears, but I had to be tough. I couldn't afford to just put up with it, my career was on the line. I told him I wanted a new chassis, a new engine and a new race engineer.

Well, he got the new chassis, but I was stuck with the engine and the engineer. Murray called me and asked me to come and test the car. I did – and it felt great, apart from the engine. We were back in business. My guess is that the old chassis, having done one and a half seasons, had simply become tired and was no longer rigid enough. Anyway, we turned up at Brands, I set pole position and walked the race from start to finish, in front of the F1 teams. We won by about half a minute, it was ridiculous. But this time it wasn't because I was pushing like crazy, as I had done at Silverstone early in the year. I just drove what felt a natural rhythm – this is how it was supposed to be. This is how it always was if I had a car as good as anyone else's. That's why I would get fuckin' angry whenever people doubted me and didn't listen to me.

Among those F1 teams in the Brands Hatch pitlane was Ron Dennis' superslick and well-financed McLaren operation, for which Niki Lauda won the following day's Grand Prix. At the other end of the pitlane was a small team called Theodore, the hobby of wealthy and eccentric Hong Kong billionaire, Teddy Yip. He may have had billions but the little man had no desire to squander them on becoming another Ron Dennis. His desires were strictly of the flesh and the passing of 70-odd years had apparently made little impact upon his libido, as he'd invariably be accompanied by a bevy of beautiful young women. The team was his VIP entry ticket into a world with a suitably glamorous backdrop for his never-ending stream of pussy. It also brought him into contact with people with whom he could do business in his trading empire, whom he wouldn't otherwise have met. He'd occasionally be photographed in front of the car, but generally had no involvement other than providing the bare minimum of a budget. This was not a serious team.

An Irishman called Sid Taylor – who'd been around the motor racing block more than a few times – ran the team on Yip's behalf. One of his duties was keeping Yip's several girl-friends apart from each other. Sometimes he failed in this and there'd be a big cat fight.

At Brands Hatch the team's car, driven by Jan Lammers, didn't go fast enough for a place on the grid. On witnessing Byrne's devastating performance in the Saturday F3 race, Taylor began to think in terms of putting Tommy in the car in place of Lammers. Two weeks later, at Hockenheim, Germany, Tommy Byrne became a Grand Prix driver.

But in the meantime, when there were no date clashes, I continued with trying to win the F3 championship with Murray. The Grands Prix meant I missed a few races but we felt we could still win it – so why not? So I'd be doing F1 one weekend, F3 the next, then back to F1 again the week after. Once, I even flew home to do the F3 race after failing to qualify for the Grand Prix. People asked if it wasn't difficult going from one very different sort of car back to another. And I would say yes it was a lot different: I could sit in the F1 car and touch the front wheels with my hands because I was sitting so far forward, whereas, in the F3 car, the front wheels were like bicycle wheels and were way up front, but it would only take me a couple of laps to get used to it.

Things weren't going too great with the Theodore in F1, so when I was coming back to do the F3 races I was even more motivated to show all the unbelieving bastards what I could do. And I was even angrier than before. Let me give you a little insight into how it felt.

I flew back from the Grand Prix in Las Vegas for the next F3 race at Silverstone. We were on the Grand Prix circuit, a track where the engine was extra important, and I still had the shitty engine I'd been complaining about for most of the year. That made me angry. I wrung the neck of the car in qualifying, yet was only on the second row because of that fucking engine. The fact that there were two guys ahead of me not even on the same planet as drivers – one of them four-eyed Dave Scott, who everyone had tipped as the pre-season favourite for the championship – made me angry too. But I knew I could still beat them in the race by using their slipstream to make up for my poor engine: it was just going to be harder work than it should've been.

So off we go, I'm running third behind Scott and soon I'm looking for a way past. I was trying to pass him about three times on every lap, yet each time he would barge me off on the grass, acting like I wasn't even there. I knew that if I ever drove like that I would get black-flagged and thrown out for dangerous driving. Yet no one seemed to mind when it wasn't me. I move to his outside as we exit the chicane – he puts me on the grass, he'd block the inside up to Stowe, so I'd go on the outside and he'd put me on the grass. Same at Club. Each time we went past the pits I would try to draw the officials' attention – but to no avail. In the end it was getting kind of funny, it was so ridiculous. I looked over at him one time with my hand in the air, telling him: 'Go on, do it again you fucking retard.' It was only because I was lifting off that there wasn't a huge crash.

But you have to know your competition. He was feeling the pressure. The pre-season favourite and I'm annihilating him in the championship, and so he was desperate. So desperate that I knew he'd make a mistake if I just kept hassling him. Sure enough, with two laps to go, he fucked up and I was through: see you, you cock-sucking four-eyed wanker, don't fuck with me! With one lap to go, I then passed the leader too. It was one of my best wins, but I was so angry with the organisers afterwards.

In the two remaining races I did enough to secure the F3 championship – despite having started on just a wing and a prayer, despite having to miss a few events to do the F1 races, despite having had to quit the team part-way through in order to get what we needed to win, despite that shitty engine and a diffi-cult engineer who didn't believe in me, who took too much notice of what I did off the track and not enough of what I was doing on it. But I wondered if it was going to make any difference. I was still haunted by that meeting early in the year with Ron Dennis. Winning the F3 championship at least guaranteed that I got to test Dennis' F1 car – that was part of the prize organised by Marlboro. So maybe I could impress Ron then and make amends?

After clinching the title a gang of us – led by Stan – went out and celebrated. A few weeks later, Murray Taylor received a visit from two guys in leather jackets – plain-clothes cops. They asked him where he'd got the money to run Tommy Byrne. They asked to see his books. They asked him if he was familiar with Stan. They showed him pictures of Stan at restaurants with me and the Italian gangsters. They asked him if Stan was financing the race team. He wasn't. But he did support me. The reason the police were interested was this: turned out Stan's motorhomes were being used by the wop gangsters to smuggle drugs. That was what the noise was when I thought I was damaging the motorhome when I stayed in it at Silverstone: it hadn't been the cab my bed was banging against, but a false compartment for the drugs.

Although he wasn't involved in the drugs, only the motorhomes, Scotland Yard had had Stan – and anyone associated with him, including me – under surveillance all year. They had even been at some of the Grands Prix I'd done and had lots of pictures of us together. Stan and around 30 others were arrested and charged. I went to one of his court dates and on the way out was stopped by a Special Branch guy who started asking me questions about Stan and wanted to know if I would come in within the next few days for an interview. 'Sure,' I said. Then, instead of driving home, I headed straight to Liverpool and got on a ferry to Dublin. I'd done nothing wrong but I knew enough about how things worked to know that I might end up incriminating myself or making things worse for Stan. I called them from Dublin and said I'd love to talk to them if they wanted to come to Ireland and do the interview. I never heard from them again.

Stan spent about three years in prison. I went to see him a couple of times. And I remember telling him: fuck those guys, you are in here and they are off scot-free, turn the fuckers in and get out of here early. 'No, Tommy I will do the time,' he replied. I felt sick to my stomach as he walked back inside for another Christmas.

CHAPTER EIGHT

Knacker to F1 in Four Years

I was approached by Theodore after the '82 British Grand Prix. I'd begun the season not even knowing if I was going to make it to F3 and here I was being offered an F1 drive – for three years, starting next weekend. It sounds good on paper doesn't it? But no one was deluding themselves that this was a top drive; it wasn't. Everyone who had driven the Theodore that year had struggled in it, it was miles off the pace of the serious teams' cars. But it was an opportunity I might not get again.

I was unsure of what to do and asked a lot of people whose opinion I respected. Most said I had to go for it. John McCambridge was one of the few that said I shouldn't, that being down the wrong end of the grid might hurt my reputation.

Then there was the matter of Ron Dennis. He still

had first option on my services. I called him, told him of the offer, asked what he thought. His reply was: 'No problem. But we at McLaren would advise you to sign for one year only with Theodore.'

I went back to Theodore, told them what Ron had said. They came back with: 'It's three years or nothing.' So I go back to Ron, tell him what they'd said. He repeated: 'We at McLaren would advise you to sign for one year only.' I then said: 'Do you at McLaren have any plans in the next three years for me, Tommy Byrne?' His reply: 'No.' I went ahead and signed the contract.

There's no way I figured in Ron's plans. I know that; I was there. It's since been claimed that I gave up a McLaren test deal to drive the Theodore. Bollocks! There was no McLaren test deal. If there had've been it would've been a no-brainer to stay there. Ron saying he had no plans for me just confirmed the impression I'd got at our fateful meeting early in the year. He had no need for a knacker from Dundalk, no matter how fast I could drive a racing car.

So Tommy went ahead and signed to three years of Theodore. Why would a little team want to secure an F1 novice for three years? Because if he turned out to be any good they could sell on his contract to a bigger team. That's exactly what had happened earlier in the year when they'd had Derek Daly on contract just when Williams found themselves in need of an experienced driver at short notice, following the out-of-the-blue retirement of their driver Carlos Reutemann two races into the season. Williams paid Theodore handsomely to release Daly – and Theodore were quick to recognise a potential source of valuable income in Tommy.

Initially I asked Theodore for $100,000 the first year, $250,000 the second year and $500,000 for the third. I knew that Frank Williams had paid Theodore quite a bit of money early in the season to get Derek Daly out of his contract with them, and I figured I was worth more than Derek, but in hindsight I definitely pitched too high! Julian Randles nearly fell off his seat laughing, then offered to pay my expenses and a percentage of any prize money. Whoopee-do!

So I got my first taste of an F1 car later in the week, testing the Theodore at Oulton Park. How was it? It was no big deal, to be honest with you. Yes, it had a lot more power but within a few laps I'd forgotten about it. It had virtually no suspension, that was the way F1 cars were in those days, and I remember noticing that without my belts fastened I could touch the front wheels from the cockpit. If you were to have a big frontal impact, your legs were going to be in a lot of peril – not that I was thinking about that. I got a feel for it pretty much straightaway and we easily broke the lap record – but this wasn't a track that F1 teams usually tested on, so that didn't mean much.

We went off to Hockenheim for the German Grand Prix. The more I worked with this team, the more I realised it was not serious. As usual, I got on great with the mechanics – they were a great bunch of guys. But the way the team was being managed was not even up to the standard of a Formula Ford team. Actually, the car wasn't diabolically bad. They had a race car and a spare. I tried them both and the spare car had much better grip in the high-speed corners, but the race car had a much stronger engine. I asked if we could put the good engine in the spare car and concentrate on that. The team manager was a guy called Julian

Randles who said 'oh, we'll do that next time.' Next time! What fucking good was that? In my reaction I may not have handled myself in a way that was going to make me friends on the team – but what the fuck was I supposed to do when these guys were just not serious and it was my reputation that was potentially going to be damaged?

So I drove the car as hard as I could but with such a shitty engine on a track with such very long straights it was a hopeless case – and I didn't qualify. It was embarrassing. The whole F1 thing – the glamour, the big occasion, the significance of the moment – all of that shit just passed me by. I was just overwhelmed with shame and frustration at being where we were – and I was already deeply pissed off with the team, Randles in particular.

One of the practice sessions was wet and in the spray of another car Didier Pironi – who had qualified on pole in the dry – crashed his Ferrari very seriously and was taken off to hospital with terrible leg injuries. Like I said, if you crashed them, your legs were going to get it. Potentially, that meant there was now a spare place on the grid, so we might get to race, after all. But Ferrari refused to withdraw Pironi's entry as a mark of respect to him – they wanted his pole position space to be left empty – and so it was still no dice. My overriding memory of that weekend isn't of some highlight in my life, but of sitting around a table in the paddock one evening and my girlfriend Edele flashing me her pussy when the others couldn't see.

Two weeks later I turned up for the Austrian Grand Prix, expecting them to have put the strong engine in the spare car. But they hadn't. I asked Randles why not. He replied, 'What would you know, you're fresh out of F3?' There was just no respect there, they'd no idea what they had in me. I knew that had I been in a McLaren or a Williams I could have gone into my first Grand Prix with every chance of winning it. I knew this – my later test with McLaren just confirmed it to anyone else who might've been interested. Randles was trying to tell me it was lack of experience on my part why their car was so slow. He actually said that if Keke Rosberg was driving it, it would be fighting for pole position, which was just ridiculous! I was beside myself with rage.

The Osterreichring at least had a lot of bends in it, unlike Hockenheim, so I could make more of a difference there. On the Saturday practice session – which, unfortunately didn't count for the grid – I was 13th fastest out of 29 cars – way, way higher than the car, or especially the team, deserved. Had I done that time in qualifying, I'd have been ahead of John Watson's McLaren. Right at the end of that session I felt a bang from the car. The car was still going, but I brought it in and told them. They checked it over but found nothing. But something was wrong, because when I then took it out for qualifying, it was nowhere near the car it had been in the morning.

I wrung the fucking neck of that car and got it onto the last row of the grid, so at least I was starting the race this time. But the embarrassment of lining up there on the back was painful. I got past a few cars on the first lap, including one of the McLarens, but they were soon able to repass me. Eventually the sidepod came adrift in one of the fast corners, altering the aerodynamics, and I was distracted watching my mirrors as the leader came to lap me – and I went off onto the grass and out of the race. So much for my first Grand Prix.

I was being interviewed on BBC radio on the Saturday and was asked didn't I find it daunting straight out of F3 racing against legends like Niki Lauda. I replied, 'Niki who?' – just as a joke – then went on to explain no, because I wasn't really in the same race as Lauda, as his car was so much faster, I would just have to do my own race. I was quite proud of the quip though, and was telling the reporter Bob Constanduros about it when he came to interview me for an F1 magazine. But when the magazine came out, there was none of the explanation, just the quote – and it just made me look like an arrogant prick. An arrogant prick at the back of the grid, what's more.

Coming on top of my problems with the management at Theodore, I was getting a reputation. Was I doing something wrong? When I looked back over all my other seasons in racing, I'd never had problems with people – but the critical difference was that I'd always been winning. Even if there was a disagreement, I could always hit back the only way I knew – by winning. That would prove my point. It had happened earlier in the year in F3 with Murray Taylor, when I had to quit the team to get him to do what was necessary to keep winning. But afterwards I was winning again and we no longer had a problem. It had been the same in Formula Ford with Van Diemen – occasionally a difference of opinion, but always I could hit back by winning. I was respected as a result.

Here, that option just wasn't there. They had no respect for me, but their car was so far off it was not possible to win, so I'd no way of hitting back. It was just this vicious circle of disrespect. I was being treated like a wanker by a bunch of wankers. This is what happens when you lose your career momentum and are no longer perceived as the big thing. I'd got all the way to F1 by my talent and personality. People usually liked me and I knew what I wanted and usually got it. That all changed when I got to F1. But not because it was F1, but because of one guy specifically at Theodore. They did not care about my talent, but had a very different agenda. I believe they just wanted to keep their jobs and it was much easier to just keep blaming the driver than to accept they were doing anything wrong.

After three great years with professionals and getting what I needed, here I was for the first time with people questioning my ability. I was not equipped for that, and I reacted aggressively. Senna would not have been treated like that because with money comes respect – and Senna wouldn't have needed to get into a situation like this anyway, because he could always buy his own options in life. Being the knacker from Dundalk didn't help. Basically, everything I had worked and struggled for since that first day at the racing school in Mondello was ruined in the space of about one month by one guy. At one point, the thought crossed my mind to have him bumped off – that's the state he had got me into. I was even quoted a price for it. In the end, I didn't do it, thank God. But there have been times when I've questioned that decision.

Helping run the team was Jo Ramirez, a really nice guy but, like Randles the team manager, he clearly had no clue about my ability. In Austria he thought he'd try to help me by getting his friend Jackie Stewart, the retired world champion, to come and talk to me about the art of driving a racing car. I stood there and politely nodded while Jackie went into transmit mode but I was absolutely furious inside. As soon as he'd finished I went and found Jo and told him not to ever again get anyone to tell me how to drive a fucking racing car. These guys just didn't understand: I was the best racing driver in the world at that time. I truly believed that then and looking back I'm still convinced I was right.

At Dijon and Monza we didn't qualify; they never did put the good engine into the better chassis. But at Las Vegas, for the final race, I scraped it onto last place of the grid. I passed my old Formula Ford 'buddy' Raul Boesel at the start and later got past Manfred Winkelhock too, but I was pushing like crazy getting that thing to do those things and eventually, after 40 laps of it, I tagged one of the walls, damaging the suspension. Actually, the race leader, Michele Alboreto, was coming up to lap me and I was distracted watching my mirrors again, making sure I kept out of his way. When I looked up I was on the dust and on the way into the wall.

Afterwards, back at the garage, someone said something they shouldn't about it and I didn't react well. I'd had it with this team of disbelieving bastards – and I told them that I wasn't ever going to get into one of their cars again, contract or no contract. I might have thrown a chair or two. I parted by telling them to turn up at Silverstone and watch me drive the McLaren. Then they might finally understand.

PART THREE:

Down The Snakes

CHAPTER NINE

The McLaren Test

So after creating such a bad impression with Ron
Dennis in our first meeting, then doing the opposite of
what he had advised me to do about racing the
Theodore – even though he wasn't offering me anything in its place – I think it was probably a bit of an
embarrassment to him that he had to give me a run in
the McLaren at the end of the year, due to a contract-
ual situation with his sponsor, Marlboro. I would guess
the last thing in the world he really wanted was for me
to shine in that test.

I was there with four other hopefuls: Thierry
Boutsen, Stefan Johansson, Quique Mansilla and Dave
Scott. I'd been out the night before with my mate. We'd
picked up a couple of girls and we brought them to the
test, which probably created a bad impression. I mean,
she looked like a whore. She wasn't, but she wore lots of

make-up and a skirt that barely covered her arse.

McLaren's star drivers of the time were Niki Lauda and John Watson, neither of whom were at the test. But the fact remains that Byrne lapped the car substantially faster than it had ever gone around Silverstone in their hands. Comparing times from different days can never be a science, as ambient temperatures have a huge effect on lap times. But even so ...

    Watson – who'd driven the car at the same venue the previous Tuesday in preparation for the test – remains astounded at Byrne's performance to this day. 'There is nothing other than phenomenal talent that can explain that lap time – that series of lap times, in fact. There is no way around explaining it. Regardless of whether it was a good day or a good set of tyres, however you shape it, it was an unbelievable *performance. I would argue actually a more impressive performance than Senna did in the equivalent test the following year, which everyone still raves about. If you could've created a driver with Tommy's enormous degree of talent and Niki's intelligence, then you'd have a driver that even Ayrton Senna would have found difficult to contain.' A conclusion that, as we've already seen, Senna may well have reached himself.*

This was the test that everybody in racing talks about whenever my name is mentioned. They know everything about it – how I told Ron Dennis his car was a piece of shit, how I screwed my career by being too cocky. Except they know nothing, because none of those things are true. Ron Dennis wasn't even at the test! It was run by Tyler Alexander. Johansson had driven the day before, when it had been a bit damp, so we couldn't really compare his times. Scott and

Mansilla did their runs the day after Boutsen and myself. On the day of my test, Boutsen drove first. He did about fifteen laps, came in, and was complaining of understeer. He was given a new set of tyres, went back out, and did 1m 10.9s. It was all conducted in a very professional way. The McLaren mechanics then set about fitting my pedals, which I'd had made up when I'd visited the McLaren factory the week before. They gave us all our own pedal sets, each with our names on them. As we each did our runs, they would have the relevant name on the side of the car. There was a lot of attention to detail.

While this was going on I was a little nervous. I felt a lot hung on this test, that I just might be able to reclaim all the damage I'd done earlier in the year in my relationship with Ron Dennis. Also, I badly wanted to show those fuckers from Theodore how wrong they were. But here was Boutsen talking about understeer and he was a guy I respected as quick. But once I got in the car my worries completely dissolved. Yes, there was some understeer, but all I did was brake a bit earlier, turn in a bit earlier and then get on the gas earlier. Result: no understeer! The car was unbelievably good. I was taking corners in fourth that in the Theodore had been third and that Boutsen had apparently been taking in third too. After just the second lap I felt that I needed to go up a gear. I was nearly flat out in fourth through Stowe, which was unbelievable. In the Theodore it hadn't even been flat in third.

By the time I came in on the old tyres I'd already gone as fast as Boutsen had on his new tyres! Then they fitted my new set. Now I was excited! I was going *four seconds* a lap faster than in the Theodore. Subtract four seconds from the Theodore's laps in the Grands Prix and I'd been right at the front. They gave my last three laps as 1m 10.01s, 1m 10.01s, 1m 10.01s. My friend Joey Greenan was there, timing me himself, and he's adamant that my last two laps were even quicker but for some reason they didn't show them. He had me down as doing 1m 9.6s on my last lap. This was on race tyres too, not qualifiers.

To me it was the simple confirmation of what I'd suspected all along. Driving a good F1 car, it was no more difficult to be competitive than driving a good FF1600 or F3 car. If I got into a good car, regardless of the formula, I was good enough to win. This test just confirmed that. Had I made my Grand Prix debut with a McLaren or a Williams, I could have been in a position to win immediately. It's not rocket science. Last year people were amazed when Lewis Hamilton was able to run at the front immediately, win races and fight for the world championship. Of course he was! He was the best driver in the best car. Twenty-five years ago, I was the best driver out there. Other people may have been amazed at the times I ran in the McLaren, but I wasn't. It was normal, it tallied with everything else I'd done whenever I was in a competitive car.

Did I tell the team anything derogatory about their car? Of course not. It was a fantastic car. I may have said something along the lines of 'Yes, there's a bit of slow corner understeer that if we could tune out I could go quicker', just in the way of feedback. They thanked me for my time and I went home.

And waited. The phone didn't ring. There was no message from Ron Dennis. Then *Motoring News* came out the following week and there was a report of the test that was a bit underwhelming and saying my 'cocky attitude' had not left a very favourable impression with the management – and it was apparent the team hadn't given a very positive account to Alan Henry, the journalist. And from that moment, any thoughts I had of my performance in the test changing my chances with McLaren were over. As far as I was concerned I'd made a bad impression with Ron Dennis earlier in the year, and they'd had to run me in the test only because of a contract with Marlboro. The fact that they still hadn't shown any interest – despite me making their car go faster than it had ever gone before – confirmed I'd no chance there.

Murray Taylor was so upset with how I'd been portrayed in the piece that he arranged a dinner with Alan Henry, me and Murray, just to show him that I really was an OK guy. It went OK but then Alan asked me which driver I compared myself to and I replied that I didn't really compare myself to anyone, but that the closest would be a mix between Alain Prost and Gilles Villeneuve – and he nearly spat his dinner out! So much for that.

About six years ago I was in the pitlane in Road America and a guy stopped me. I recognised him from somewhere. He said, 'Hi Tommy, how the hell are you and what have you been up to all these years?'

'Oh, just teaching and coaching,' I said.

'Yeah, you were so fast that day when you tested the McLaren and you did not even have the best car.'

What was he talking about, I asked. I'd had the same car as Boutsen, who'd just got out of it.

'Yeah,' he said, 'but when I was changing your pedals I was told not to give you full throttle.'

Well that got me thinking: could that be true? It would explain why I started using fourth gear instead of third – and probably why I was nearly flat out at Stowe, because the car would be approaching the turn so much slower. But I am pretty sure McLaren would never have done something like that – or given me the wrong times. They are much too professional. And why would they even care about Tommy Byrne? I would have preferred not to have run into Tony Vandungen that day, as I'd long ago put that whole test behind me, and he re-ignited my feelings about it.

So let's ask Vandungen himself what he recalls of that day. 'Well, it was an awfully long time ago! But yes, my recollection is that we were instructed to give Tommy less than full throttle – and only Tommy, not the others.' Why might that have been? 'I honestly don't believe it was to screw Tommy, more to protect him and the car. I recall having spoken to him at the Austrian Grand Prix, when he was driving the Theodore, and it was looking like he'd be getting the McLaren test. He was very cocky, totally confident about how fast he was going to be in the McLaren. And at the test he was the same. I think there was a feeling, probably from Tyler Alexander, who was running the test, that his attitude might just make him liable to crash the car. This wasn't a show car, but it was an active race car, one of the team's pukka cars, and damaging it would not have been good. We didn't feel the other guys were as aggressive about how quick they were going to be, but with Tommy we had a bit of a concern, especially as he was going out after Boutsen, so would have a time to aim for, so we detuned the car a little. You just adjust the amount of throttle available by screwing the throttle stop – the stop that the pedal comes up against – up a little. You then look down the engine's inlet trumpets, and with the throttle against the stop, if you can see any of the throttle slide showing, you haven't got full throttle. It would only take a few seconds. He then went very fast regardless and we all had a good laugh about it, thinking just how fast he could have gone. Tommy was one of those drivers, a bit like Tony Stewart today, who is superconfident, aggressively so – and then goes out on the track and delivers, totally backing up his attitude.'

Then there was the matter of the lap times. The 1m 10.01s they showed on the board was superimpressive. But two witnesses who were watching very closely, Joey Greenan and John Uprichard, two Irish racing stalwarts who had come to watch Tommy's test from the sidelines, are adamant he was lapping faster than that. Greenan, the driver who had spotted Byrne's talent over five years earlier, takes up the story. 'John was working for Van Diemen, and we'd arrived there in the factory truck. John was just timing Tommy off his wristwatch and it didn't seem to tally with the times the team were putting on the pit board. So he sent me back to the truck to get the proper stopwatch. I began timing him and he was going up to 1s faster than what they were showing. I went to the team and asked them why the hell weren't they showing the proper times? By the end he was in the 1m 9s. His last three laps I had down as 1m 9.9s, 1m 9.7s, 1m 9.6s.'

Even if we just take the 'official' times, this was the quickest the ground effect McLaren MP4/1 ever went around Silverstone – by a substantial margin. The cool air of autumn would have made for faster times than the hot July air of mid-season, the engine would have been breathing more oxygen, perhaps the team had fitted longer gear ratios in the car to protect the engine during the test and had therefore inadvertently geared it perfectly for the more potent engine performance, thus explaining some of it. But some of that would be negated anyway if there was not 100 per cent throttle opening. Besides, as Watson says, no matter which way you try to explain it, which version of events you go with, it remained a sensational performance.

'Yes, Tommy was sensational that day,' says Greenan, 'but then again, it was only what I would have expected. Thierry Boutsen was a fairly good driver but he was no Tommy Byrne. In terms of talent Tommy was an Ayrton Senna, no two ways about it. Had Ron Dennis taken him on, had his face fit there, I've got no doubts at all that he would have been a multiple world champion.'

Dennis himself recalls Tommy with something that, 25 years on, sounds suspiciously like fondness: 'Good old Tommy Byrne. What a character – and what a talent. I think most people who saw him race would agree that he had what it takes, in terms of the gift of naked car control, to go all the way. But perhaps he lacked some of the other necessary ingredients – the steely determination, the unflinching focus and the towering ambition that mark out the true greats. As a result, Tommy's career has to be viewed as one of under-achievement – if only in the context of his very considerable natural ability. He won the 1982 British Formula Three championship well enough, though, and tested for McLaren at the end of that year. He was clearly quick – and, had his undoubted talent been matched by an equal quantity of the other traits a top racing driver requires, then he might well have become a true great, and I would have been delighted if he'd done so at the wheel of a McLaren. Sadly, it wasn't to be.'

Whatever really happened that October day in 1982, it came to define Tommy's life. It was the moment when his destiny path split from glittering awards, from fame, from fortune – to some other life. In recognising the moment as that, he may even have made it a self-fulfilling prophecy. It *hit him hard. It's difficult not to think he was never quite the same again.*

At the end of the year there was a big awards ceremony, where I was to be presented with my trophy for winning the F3 championship. I was in a terrible state of mind. As far as I was concerned it was all over for me. I'd done all I could on my talent and my personality and now the damage done by my relationship with Ron Dennis, and to my reputation by the Theodore, meant I was all washed up. I could not see any way forward. This should have been my moment of triumph – picking up my F3 award, looking forward to a great F1 career. But there was no great F1 career that I could see. It was gone. That woman had been right – I was the knacker from Dundalk, nothing more than a knacker. What was there to lose now? From now on, I'd decided, it was party time. I might not have made it, but racing was still a great life. No one questioned you when you were the bollocks, no one was prepared to tell you when you were being a cunt. From now on, I was in freefall from a long way up, enjoying the wild ride down.

On the morning of the awards ceremony day a friend offered me a huge bag of cocaine. He said a friend had given it to him, he'd snorted just a little bit and he was up all night. He'd never had coke before and he'd decided after this that he didn't like it. The state of mind I was in, I was up for it and said 'Hell yeah!' I'd tried a little earlier in the year and it seemed to clear my head, seemed to help me make decisions. So I laid out two ginormous lines and snorted them. Soon I felt a whole lot better. 'Here I am, the F3 champion, going to the ball' full of myself. Eventually,

I find myself sitting at the dinner table at the awards do with the guys from Murray Taylor Racing, my girlfriend Edele and my buddy, Stuart Dent. The food arrived, it looked great – but I was too 'excited' to eat. I was flying, telling jokes at a million miles an hour, the life and soul of the party. No one knew I'd been snorting coke all day. Then came my turn to go to the stage and receive my prize. I vaguely remember applause and some trophies and everyone high-fiving me on my way back to the table. I can't recall who presented me with the trophy – but I'm told it was Niki Lauda.

When I got back to the table I had to tell someone about the coke, so I told Stuart. We went to the toilet and I showed him this huge bag. He took a look at it and said, 'That's not coke, it's speed.' I shrugged. Big deal, what's the difference?

After the evening finished I went back to Edele's place and after about two hours of not performing, I confessed why. She went berserk! Then threw me out, told me we were finished. It was about 3am and I couldn't think of where I could go. So I went to the guy that gave me the 'coke'. He said he hoped I hadn't taken too much because he was up all night with his heart racing. Anyway, I lay down for five minutes and it felt like five hours – and my heart was trying to come through my chest. I couldn't rest, so I left, got in my car and drove all the way to Norfolk, to the cottage I was still renting from Angie and Ralph Firman and where my ex-mechanic, Dave Meehan – who was Senna's mechanic by then – was staying.

I crawled into bed and stayed there for the next three days, depressed and crying. My life was over, there was nothing to live for. My career was finished, my girlfriend had dumped me. I'd worked hard to get to F1 and now it was over before it had barely started. I couldn't tell anyone what was wrong, not even my friend Dave. Eventually I told Angie Firman and she helped talk it through. I now realise it was a depression fuelled by speed, but it's given me a real appreciation of the horrors of depression. Afterwards I vowed never to do speed again. But speed wasn't the root of it. My fucked career was.

CHAPTER TEN

Travelling Backwards,
Looking West

Tommy never again drove an F1 car. He was no longer on that career ladder. In fact it was arguable if he was on any career ladder. All he'd determined was the geographic location of where he wanted to race next now the dream had turned sour. The romantic notion of America, the big place far across the water from Ireland, where anything was possible, where you could be anything you wanted, still held a powerful draw – the promise of refuge from the hard-edged unsympathetic world of F1, which requires you to buy into its values, its social mores, if you're to be accepted. In America you can be anything you want. In America Tommy could be himself, could get over the confidence-bruising brush with F1, could enjoy the company of a clique of other refugees from the European racing scene, many of them Irish. Had Tommy had a manager worth a light at this time, he'd have a) built his confidence back up and probably aggressively pursued

options in Europe to get him back on the F1 ladder, or fail-
ing that, b) have brought him to America amid a lot of hype
and talked him into a good ride, not just whatever any guy
Tommy stumbled across might have offered him.

Eventually I picked myself up. The F1 dream may have
been over but I had this idea I wanted to go to
America. It had started when I was a kid watching John
Wayne movies. We only had two TV channels, RTE 1
and RTE 2, and every holiday and Christmas it was
movie day and I loved John Wayne, knew that I would
go to America someday. I nearly went as a welder after
I was fired from CRV, but that was before I went to the
Mondello race school, which kinda changed my plan.
I'd always wanted to live there, I had this big romantic
view of it, like a lot of Irish people seem to. I started
thinking in terms of trying to get a race seat out there.
But Eddie Jordan changed my mind.

As a fellow Irish guy in England I'd got to know
Eddie pretty well. He'd given up trying to be a race
driver by around this time, and was getting himself
established as a team owner. I was often over at his
race shop at Silverstone – it was sort of an Irish racing
hang-out. Murray Taylor, my entrant in '82, was his
neighbour, so we were always around each other.
Eddie persuaded me to do the '83 European F3 series
with his team. I was very depressed at the time. I knew
it was all over for me, that I was no longer the big
thing on account of the Theodore chapter and also
my not hitting it off with Ron Dennis. Anyway, Eddie
was able to talk me round, made me feel that if I could
do well there might be a way back into F1. He always
did have the gift of the gab. He had some sponsorship
from Yokohama tyres, which was good but also bad –

because it meant we had to use their tyres and at the time they weren't as good as the Michelins nearly everyone else was using. But what the fuck? I was racing.

It started off well. In fact, we were leading the championship at around halfway through the season. It was a good fun time, and helped get me out of the doldrums. I got on great with my mechanics, Shay Campbell and Jeremy, and we had some great races. The first win came at the Österreichring and was quite a big deal because it was Gerhard Berger's home track and a circuit that I really loved. He qualified on the front row with me right behind him, but I made a poor start and was about fifth into the first corner. I picked them all off in the next few laps until there was only Gerhard ahead of me and I passed him about three-quarters of the way through and won. He claims he put me to bed the night before. Maybe he did, I don't remember. But I did have a lot of fun with him.

At Monaco, for the Grand Prix support race, I'd qualified on the second row but on the dummy start I broke first gear. I thought I'd be swamped into the first corner for the race start, but actually, with a bit of weaving, I managed to drop just two places. Other than the start, you needed first gear at Loews hairpin and one other turn, so I was just braking early – I could hear all the others up my ass as I did this – then slipping the clutch in second. Driving with the car like this, I passed two others and finished third. I rate it as one of my best ever races. I did all my passing into Mirabeau, the corner just past the Tip Top bar, where my good friend Stuart was watching, hanging over the barriers like a madman. He disappeared for a couple of laps then came back. I asked him after the race where he went, and he told me, 'Oh I had to go get another beer.' We always had fun at the Tip Top, even the year before when James Hunt had tried to pick up my girlfriend, Edele. I rate this as one of my best ever races. I was a little disappointed that I did not get to stand on the podium because in the F3 race only the winner gets up there. But I guess everyone had stopped watching me by then anyhow.

Misano was a track I'd never seen before, anti-clockwise too. We had some Yokohama qualifying tyres and in the first session I put it on pole, but had to sit out the next session because they hadn't brought enough tyres. But still, no one beat our time, so I was starting from pole. We didn't have any race tyres. All we had was another set of the quallie tyres. We figured we'd lead a few laps and then fall backwards down the pack. I took off in the lead but actually the tyres were holding up OK. By the end they were just about finished, but I was still able to hold Pierluigi Martini off to win the race.

This is the race that sends Jordan into streams of superlatives about Byrne's talent. 'He'd never seen the place before, it was anti-clockwise, a tricky old place to learn. The pole time came on something like his third flying lap of the place! Just unbelievable. I've no idea how that was possible – but that was Tommy for you. He'd do things that defied logic. In terms of raw talent he's up there with the greatest, with the Sennas and the Schumachers. Then the next minute he'd have you tearing your hair out.' E.J. then goes on to tell a tale about the reason for missing the second session was that Tommy was nowhere to be found – and was actually having a liaison with a lady when he should have been in the car. 'Completely false,' asserts Tommy. 'That's just the way tales about me seem to grow. It's half-remembered and mixed up with something else and before you know it I have this reputation. No, the reason we missed the second session was purely to do with the tyres.' Shay Campbell, Tommy's mechanic at the time, remembers it exactly as Tommy tells it.

Anyway, we led the championship at halfway, ahead of Berger, Martini and Emanuelle Pirro. They were good drivers but I didn't consider any of them rivals. They weren't at the same level, just as no one had been during my '82 title year or in FF2000 or FF1600. The only guy I'd encountered so far that I could see was at a similar level was Senna – and we'd never raced against each other. But the time came in that '83 season when we did.

Unfortunately, it coincided with a problem we began having with the car. It seemed to happen overnight. We turned up for the Silverstone round of the European championship and the top British F3 guys like Senna and Martin Brundle – who E.J. was running in the UK – took part in it too. Through the fast turns there the car was just terrible, would just snap into a big oversteer. Even corners that were normally easily flat I was having to lift for – it was ridiculous. I even crashed at Stowe during testing, trying to go through there at my normal speed. Basically, the car was like this for the rest of the year no matter what we tried with it. It was unbelievably frustrating. Here was my chance to race Senna at last and the fuckin' car was playing up. Brundle won the race, Senna crashed and I had a shit-fight just to finish a distant second.

In the following races we began falling backwards in the championship and Eddie seemed to lose interest.

My mechanics gave it 100 per cent trying to trace the problem but we never did. I begged Eddie to let me have just two laps in Brundle's car, just so I could prove it wasn't me. But that was understandably vetoed by Martin's mechanic, Alistair. That was it basically. I knew there was going to be no F1 comeback for me.

Years later I was talking to Ross Cheever. He was telling me of this really ill-handling car he'd bought from Eddie at the end of '83 and how the thing would just snap into oversteer in the fast corners. And then how he climbed into another car just to check, and was suddenly flying, so they established that it was a problem with the car. They then found that the side-pods were delaminating and not supporting the down-force. As soon as they put new sidepods on it, it flew. The sidepods were the one thing we didn't change.

This sounds like a different guy to the one twelve months earlier, the one that had quit his championship-leading team in order to get what he needed, who had no intention of doing anything other than winning in front of the F1 teams. One year on, in much the same situation with an undefined technical problem, he just lets the matter slide, accepts he's going nowhere. Suddenly, Ayrton Senna really didn't have much to worry about. Looking back, the lack of response after the sensational McLaren test seems to have finally finished off Tommy's ambition, drive and focus, already damaged from the Theodore episode. Whatever, there was plenty of partying to be done ...

Eddie was also acting as my manager at this time. He was pretty tight with Marlboro, who'd sponsored him on and off for years. He said there was a chance he could get me onto the Marlboro junior driver scheme, which basically meant about £5,000 and a Marlboro jacket and bag that told everyone you were one of the select few. It came with a special services contract, was very prestigious, and could pay off big time some time down the line when they were placing their drivers. I was constantly on at Eddie: 'Did you talk to Marlboro? Did you talk to Marlboro?' Eventually, at Silverstone for the Grand Prix support race, he produced 'the jacket'. It was a pukka Marlboro jacket alright, but there was no contract, no money. 'Where's the rest of the stuff Eddie?'

'Oh, be off with ya, ya cunt. I have it in me office.' But I still didn't quite believe him. All I had was a jacket. 'There's Ron Dennis over there,' E.J. said. 'Go in your Marlboro jacket and say hello to him.'

Well, given my history with Ron, that was quite something Eddie was asking me to do. But he was my manager, I ought to listen to him. So I walk over to Ron with my special jacket, just like Ron's special Marlboro jacket, because they'd been his sponsor for years. Ron would know who was on special services contracts and who wasn't, and as I was walking towards him, not really trusting that Eddie had got me the deal, I began to feel like I was an impostor. Well, it was too late now as I was right up to him and had just stuck out my hand and begun to say, 'Hello Ron, how are you?' when, before I could finish, he just turned around and began talking to someone else. I turned around in my bright red Marlboro jacket now with a face to match and looked across at E.J. – who just sort of grimaced then looked away. I never did see any contract. It was just a jacket.

But that weekend – when E.J. had entered me with the Euro car for the British Grand Prix support race and I'd again been nowhere, still struggling with its evil handling – had its compensations. After the race I was hanging around shooting the breeze with my old entrant Murray Taylor and Davy Jones, who had replaced me in Murray's team. Davy was talking to this beautiful girl, Amanda, who had turned up with another driver, Mario Hytten. Davy invited us all, including Amanda, back to his place. He was renting the house of Derek Daly, the Irish driver who'd been in F1 the previous year but who was now racing in America. Davy shared the renting of this house with Joe Stoop, who was Murray Taylor's brother-in-law. You keeping up? It's kind of incestuous, I know. Murray and his wife lived next door. Joe – who worked for Murray – had previously been married to the twin sister of Murray's wife but they'd now split up. At the time I lived about twenty minutes away in Milton Keynes but I was always round at Davy and Joe's.

So after the race we're all there and having a bit of a party. I was in the kitchen, cooking, and Amanda comes in with her skintight riding trousers. She was gorgeous. She walks up behind me and starts fondling me! I could not believe it! These things never happened to me! We started kissing and then I took her upstairs. We were on the landing kissing again when Davy shouts up, 'Hey, she's with me. I brought her here you randy bastard!' So we broke off, I came down the stairs and saw Davy take her into his room, the lucky bastard. I went home with blue balls.

I went back around there the next day and it was just Joe and Amanda there. Joe took me to one side to explain that she'd been with Davy and Joe – together. I grabbed her hand, took her upstairs and continued where we'd left off in the first room I came to, which was Derek Daly's office. As the moment of climax came I looked up – and there was a picture of Derek smiling down at me!

She just wanted sex all the time – from any of us. In between times she'd cook and clean the house. It was like every man's dream come true. But eventually Davy and I began to tire of how the house always smelt of sex. One day I'd been down to London and as I got back to my Milton Keynes flat I was surprised to hear music from inside. I opened the door and there was Amanda – and the place was spotless. I asked her what she was doing here and she said, 'Oh Joe and Davy said you wanted me to come stay with you?' Oh, did they? I didn't really want her to stay so I said I'd drive her back to her mum's, which was about 120 miles up north. I did so, said hello to her mum, and none of us ever saw her again. We'd all had a great time but we learned that sometimes, when you get what you always thought you wanted, you find you don't really want it at all.

Once it was clear I wasn't going back to F1 I was still hankering after America. I got a call from a guy called Kerry Agipiou, who was running a Formula Atlantic team in the American championship. He asked if I wanted to race for him at Riverside, California? I jumped at the chance and flew out there. His team was a real family operation – Kerry, his wife, his brother and sons. I loved them, there was a great atmosphere, even though they were just getting by. They were running another car for the woman racer, Desire Wilson. I tried the car and it was on the wrong springs and needed a stiffer anti-roll bar.

They borrowed the springs from another team but Kerry couldn't locate the roll bar we needed. But I was looking at Desire's car and realised she had the exact bar that I needed. So when she disappeared for a while I nicked it from her car and put it on mine (sorry, Desire), and fitted mine on hers. We managed to qualify it in sixth, but the biggest problem was the tired old engine in the back. I managed to talk Kerry into getting a proper engine for the race. I got a great start right down the middle; it was a marginal jump-start but I got away with it and was up to third place. I had Michael Andretti one side of me and Rogelio Rodriguez on the other – and we went through turn nine like that, three abreast at about 150mph, fantastic. We continued like this, three abreast, past the start-finish line with me in the middle of a Mexican/American sandwich, until we came up to turn two, a flat out turn with room for only one car, but there was nobody lifting off. It was a game of chicken and I must admit I was the first chicken to lift off. Andretti took the lead but ran off the track a couple of turns later, which left me with a big lead over Rogelio. Then the engine blew. I felt bad for Kerry but they were all very excited, as they'd never run up at the front before.

Kerry had me back again for the next race, Sears Point, a track I loved. Andretti won, Moreno was second and I was third with an ill-handling car. It turned out after the race we found that the rear anti-roll bar was broken. I guess karma had got me for stealing it in the first place. They were a great bunch, they gave me a break into the American racing scene, and when Kerry was running cars in the ARS series a few years later, I was the first guy he called. Kerry is definitely one of the good guys in racing.

At the end of the year Gary Anderson asked me to

race his Anson at the Macau Grand Prix, a sort of F3 world championship event at the end of the season, and a great place to let off steam. Gary had designed and built his own car and was trying to get the company up and running, but the money was very tight. So there was never much testing, never much money for the best tyres etc. But it was a good little car – and I qualified it in the top ten and ran towards the front in the race after a good start until something broke. Senna won the race.

Everybody went out and partied that night, including all the drivers. Senna even joined us and started ordering shots of something and slamming them on the table then knocking 'em back. He was soon as shitfaced as the rest of us. Then, without warning, he left without paying his bill. Then all the other guys left until I was the only one there, but I didn't have the money to pay anything. So I just gave them Senna's room number.

I spent the '84 season racing in Europe again with Gary's Anson. We got the odd good result but with such limited funds it was a struggle.

It was around this time that I met Giovanna Amati. We were doing a race at Enna, in Italy, and after the race myself and Michael Roe were at a pool and Giovanna was there. I'd seen her around the circuit as she was racing in F3 but this was the first time I'd spoken to her. She was with her friend (who later went on to become a princess). We were having some wine and a good old time, then I threw her in the pool a couple of times, then I had to rescue her. I gave her my number and went back to England. A couple of days later I got a phone call from her: 'Ello Tomy, ees Giooovvvaaana,' in her Italian-English. 'How are you?

It is my birthday on Saturday and I am having a party and I would like you to come to Sardinia.'

'Giovanna, I would love to come but I am really busy this week and I don't think that I could get away.' Translation: I had no money. But she persisted until eventually I had to tell her, 'Giovanna, I have no money.'

'It is no problem,' she says in her raspy voice. 'There will be a ticket for you at Heathrow airport on Friday and I will pick you up at Sardinia airport tomorrow night.' I hung up. Wow, I guess I was going to Sardinia. Better get some laundry done.

She was there, as promised, to pick me up. Sardinia is an island off Italy where all the wealthy Italians have summer homes. It turned out Giovanna was wealthy, very wealthy. When we got to the house the party was in full swing. I felt a little awkward at first, among all the rich people, but after a couple of drinks I was fine, telling my jokes and just having a great old time. When I woke up the next morning the clothes I'd worn the night before were laundered, ironed and folded at the foot of the bed. I guess Giovanna's maid did them early in the morning. And that was the way it was to be every morning: laundry done, breakfast in bed if we wanted. I could get used to this! For the next six months Giovanna would fly me to Rome or Sardinia and we ate in all the best restaurants. She was a good friend of the F1 driver Elio De Angelis. I remember being in his parents' house in Sardinia watching him on TV racing in a Grand Prix.

Giovanna had a great body but she was a very angry person. When we went for meals with her rich friends she would slip me a couple of hundred bucks under the table to pay for me and her, and I started to feel bad about it. I told her at this stage that I would be leaving for America soon, as I felt this was my best career move. She didn't take it well. 'Why you have to go to America?' she demanded.

'To make some money,' I replied.

'You can stay here and you will not have to worry about money.'

But I felt like a kept man. Giovanna was actually a very good driver. Her only problem was, instead of wanting to win she was satisfied just because she'd beaten some men. I think the last conversation I had with her was when I was in America. On the phone I was explaining to her to about how to get a good start in her next F3 race. 'Giovanna, you need to hold the revs higher with that VW engine or it will die on the line.'

'Is this all you have to fucking tell me?' Oh well. I had a lot of good times with her.

Gary Anderson, a fellow Irishman who later went on to become an F1 technical director with Jordan and Jaguar – a tough, no-bullshit sort of guy – liked having Tommy as his driver. 'He was one of very few I've worked with that got the absolute maximum from the car, so that you know if you make a change to the car, good or bad, you would see it reflected immediately in the lap time. I've worked in F1 with drivers who, after you change something, say 'oh, it's better, it feels more comfortable' but they're doing the same lap time as before! That's no bloody good! It's not supposed to be comfortable. If it's comfortable you're not pushing hard enough. That was one thing you never got from Tommy. He was fantastically naturally gifted. You could see that just by watching him on the track – it was very like how Lewis Hamilton looks in the car today, just totally in control.

Tommy was as good as anyone, but he lacked the last little bit of focus. He'd come from nothing to become a kingpin and he was enjoying that so much I think the focus just slipped away. It's easy to do. At Donington he'd been quickest in the first session, then we had a problem with the car and while it was being fixed he borrowed my car to go back to the hotel for a liaison with a girl. The car was fixed by the time the second session started – but there was no Tommy. He claimed my car had run out of fuel. Maybe it had, but if he'd been properly focused he wouldn't have chosen that moment to give a girl a seeing-to.'

Not quite true, that bit. Yes, I did go back with my girl-friend to the hotel when the car wasn't ready, on the understanding that they'd get me when it was looking almost ready to go. And yes, we might have been doing the business when the knock came on the door. But there was a bit of a mix up over which hotel we were at and that's the only reason I was a little late – but even then, I was in the car in time for the start of the session.

'But the talent – that was something special,' continues Anderson. 'There was one time where qualifying for the Monaco F3 race was held at Paul Ricard for some reason. There wasn't time on the Monaco programme for F3 qualifying, so the grid was decided a few weeks earlier at this Ricard session. We got there and it was pouring with rain, and no one was going out – and the circuit guys said they were postponing the session, probably until the next day but that, in the unlikely event of it drying out today, they might try to squeeze it in then. So Tommy and I went off to a nearby beach cafe. I ordered an Irish coffee but the guy didn't know how to make them. So I told him how to

do it – but he kept getting it not quite right! And so he'd
have to try again. It ended up me and Tommy had about
thirty of them over the course of the afternoon. Then I look
outside and notice that there's steam rising from the road
and the sun's blazing bright. 'Quick Tommy, let's get back.
They're probably going to run the session.' As we got there
we could hear the F3 engines already out on track. So Tommy
gets changed into his overalls, I warm up the car, strap him
in and out he goes. He does three, maybe four, laps then
comes in and says 'I can't even see where the track's going.
I've got to stop.' He qualified in the top ten, less than 1s
off pole.'

No! Not true either! I'd not been drinking as many
coffees as Gary. I was perfectly OK.

The race at Monaco turned out pretty good, after a
difficult start – just like the previous year. This time
the plugs fouled on the grid and I got away last. But
Gary had made a tweak to the springing of the car,
once he'd found out a bit more about the tyres we
were running, and as soon as I got going I could feel
that it had really worked. The car felt good and I
began catching and passing people. Well, I came from
20th on the grid to finish fourth.

Cheering from a hotel balcony overlooking the Loews
Hairpin, was a well lubricated and very happy Irish contin-
gent, as Tommy gained one position after another. Chief
among their number was John Hines, a Dublin entrepreneur
who had backed the career of another Irish racer, David
Kennedy. He'd contributed a little to the running costs of
Gary's car here, his Group Waterworks sticker on the rear
wing, so he was thrilled. One thing led to another and
Tommy's American dream took a step closer to reality. The F1

dream was well and truly dead and buried now.

John Hines is one of the nicest guys in racing and has helped me out many times over my career. He just loves racing and being involved. Well, that Monaco weekend an American entrant called Bill Boynton was hanging with John and was there in the middle of it all as the Irish guys were getting excited about my race. It just so happened that Bill was running a Formula Vee car in the States and wasn't sure about his driver.

It was little wonder Boynton's thoughts turned to Tommy. On top of his dramatic Monaco F3 race, Boynton's Super Vee team had been one of those Tommy had blown away when he'd made his Super Vee debut earlier that year at Long Beach. Super Vee was approximately an American equivalent of F3, with slightly more powerful engines. It was a market Gary Anderson was keen to break into with his Anson chassis. Gary takes up the story of the Long Beach race.

'I had a guy in Chicago acting as sales agent and he prepped a car for Tommy to do the Long Beach race in. We went to Sears Point to test it and we weren't particularly quick. Then the guy says not to worry because for Long Beach we'd have the pukka Super Vee tyres! He'd had us testing on Formula Ford slicks, which were way too soft in their construction for a Super Vee. No wonder we'd been slow! Tommy lost his rag with him at this point. Anyway, we went to Long Beach and Tommy put it on pole by over 0.7s. But he'd never done a rolling start before and messed it up. He was 12th at the end of the first lap but started coming through the field. Eventually he retired after he and Arie Luyendyk collided while fighting for the lead. But we'd created a big impression. We were so much faster that they assumed the car was illegal. We were protested about

five times through the weekend, and every protest was thrown out.'

Bill had been involved in the sport in the 1960s, supporting the driver Ken Miles, who was then killed testing a car. So Bill had drifted away from the sport but had been brought back in by a Super Vee driver called Mike Hooper. Bill got Colin Bennett – who used to be an F1 mechanic – to run the team for him, but they were getting no results. Bill Boynton hadn't got involved to finish sixth, he wanted to be winning. Hooper was blaming Bennett and Bennett was blaming Hooper. So I got a phone call from Bennett asking if I'd come and drive a second car alongside Hooper at Trois Rivieres, Canada. Expenses plus a percentage of the prize. Not a mega deal, but an introduction into the American racing scene, which is where I saw my future.

I arrived at Trois Rivieres and met up with Bennett in the hotel bar, where he introduced me to Bill Boynton and Bill's young wife, Susie. Next day I saw the track for the first time, a fabulous street circuit. I met the team and started asking the normal questions: what spring rates have we got on, what ride height, how much rake, what gears are we running? Routine stuff. Yet I wasn't really getting the answers. Everyone was vague or didn't know. So I tried the car in first practice. There was a lot wrong with it and I was only fifth quickest. So I came up with a long job list. After years working with shit-hot professional people like Ralph Firman and Gary Anderson, I'd picked up a lot of knowledge about set-up, and if I had to, I could race-engineer myself, just give me a good mechanic.

It was a ground-effect Ralt, much as I'd been used to in F3. You had to run them really low to make them work. I asked them to lower the ride height. They told me the problem with that was you'd wear out the wood on the underbody. So replace the wood, I said. In Europe we'd change the wood at least twice per week-end. Do you want to win, I asked, or do you want to save $100 in wood?

Then I asked for stiffer springs. There was a prob-lem with that too. After a big argument with Bennett I got the stiffer springs. As they took the old ones off I could see they weren't even the same side-to-side.

After a lot of hassle I got the car somewhere in the ballpark, even if there was still a lot of work to do, and in the race I finished second. Bill and Susie were over the moon. I'd made two new friends and up on the rostrum told them there was still a lot of work to do if they wanted to win. They asked me to come back and do another race at the end of the year, in Las Vegas, and I said I'd love to.

Before I left, I asked Colin Bennett for my exp-enses. He said he'd send them. I told him I needed them now, as I didn't have any money to get back oth-erwise. He said I was a professional driver so I should have my own money. I was losing my patience and said, 'Are you going to pay me now or do I go and ask Bill for it.' He paid me but I had the feeling I was going to have problems with him.

I went back later in the year and raced for Bill and Susie at Las Vegas. Susie was a big part of the deal because if she didn't like you, you wouldn't be driving for Bill. She liked me and I think Colin Bennett suspected as much. Bill was just getting started again and had big plans. He said he wanted me as part of them. I finished fifth – shitty car, shitty team, shitty engine – and we all had drinks late into the night. Bill went to bed, leaving the rest of us in the bar and Susie confided to me that Colin Bennett thought me and her were sleeping together. We weren't, but here I was, doing nothing wrong, and a shit-fight was starting. So I just went back to England and forgot about Bill and Susie – I didn't have the energy for a power struggle with Colin Bennett.

But I'd at least got a taste of racing and living in America. My friend Calvin Fish was already out there, and so were a contingent of Irish drivers: Bernard Devaney, Derek Daly and Michael Roe. Also part of that scene were two guys I became really friendly with, the Scottish driver Jim Crawford and the black American driver, Willy T. Ribbs. Michael and Jim were driving in the Can Am series for Don Walker, a rich Texan who owned the whole series as well as his team. The prize money was fantastic and Michael was winning virtually everything. In 1985 I stayed with Michael and his wife Gaye at their home in Dallas and I'd go along to the Can Am races, hoping to pick something up. I'd a lot of racing friends out there so I'd no trouble finding a couch to sleep on. I loved it, the weather was fantastic, lots of parties by the pool and the girls were gorgeous. I was determined to stay.

Michael was a big help, although I never did get to drive with him in Can Am, as I'd hoped. But he asked if I'd share a Buick he was racing at Daytona and even paid for my ticket to get there. It broke when I was driving it. Whatever. I was beginning a racing career in America.

September 20, 1984

Dear Marshall:

I am delighted to learn that you have returned to
the racing circuit.

Nancy joins me in wishing you all the best in your
endeavors. God bless you.

Sincerely,

Ronald Reagan

Mr. Marshall Robbins

West Bloomfield, Michigan

CHAPTER ELEVEN

The Clown's Bitch

The clown's bitch. That's all I was after it had all turned to crap: a piece of amusement for a monstrously rich madman.

It had started when I bumped into Willy T. Ribbs tail-end of 1985. I liked him. We had a lot in common. He was the black racing driver that was beat down in America, I was the knacker that was beat down in England. Not to mention that we were both pretty cocky.

Willy introduced me to a guy called Marshall Robbins, big shot, in his thirties, throwing money around like it's going out of fashion, wants a driver to share his car in the three-hour IMSA race. I end up driving for his Spirit of Detroit team full-time in '86. Turns out he's a manic-depressive. His father, Jim Robbins, had invented and patented a seat belt part that all of Detroit used: whoo-hoo, let's buy the world! But he'd cut Marshall off – I guess because he was unstable – and so Marshall became a DJ. But in '75 Marshall's Dad, mother and sister were killed in a plane crash and Marshall inherited everything. Before he was just a crazy fucker, but now he'd got money he was 'eccentric'.

He read the book of revelations but interpreted them his way. One of the things he came up with was he was going to be President of America in 1992. He began prepping his girlfriend Jacques to be First Lady. He used to carry a picture of himself with Ronald Reagan. Whenever he got stopped for speeding he'd produce the picture, a picture that had probably cost him a couple of hundred thousand dollars. For a while he became convinced that the CIA had managed to get an implant in his chin in order to track him – because obviously they knew he was going to become President.

Sometimes he drove the race car. Once, in Road Atlanta, he came into the pits to tell his mechanic that Paul Newman was up a tree at one of the corners spying on him, and that he wasn't going back out until the mechanic went and got him down. Usually, though, he hired others to drive.

In fact, he hired others for everything, including being his friend. He'd have this big entourage around him and they were paid well, because that's the only way anyone would hang round with the crazy bastard. Every room in each of his houses was wired for sound and if he couldn't sleep, neither could anyone else. He'd just put on the music and everybody had to join in the party. He'd stay awake for days on end, music blasting from every room in the house. They all laughed at his jokes, agreed with his bad ideas – me included, I'm afraid. I was just going whichever way the wind blew by now; trading on the only thing I knew how to do well. If I ever disagreed, or baulked, he'd say, 'Tommy, you're self-destructing' – a regular phrase, which, when translated, meant I was about to lose my job.

One of the entourage was a guy called Ricky, who was a pro singer that Marshall was sponsoring. He used to sing at the September Club, a real exclusive place in West Palm Beach, about thirty minutes from Boca Raton, where Marshall had a place on the water. He kept his two speedboats there. One was liveried in American red, white and blue; the other was jet black, his 'Guido' boat. 'Guido' was an imaginary character of his that he would sometimes slip into. Whenever he was Guido he would dress all in black: big black hat, long black overcoat, like he was an Italian mobster.

One day, mid-season, Marshall decided to take us all on a cruise. I was pretty excited till I discovered he'd just booked us a place on an old people cruise. As well as Marshall, the First Lady in Waiting was there, Ricky, myself – about ten of us in all. Marshall flew into West Palm Beach the night before in a Lear Jet he'd hired for $30,000. On the day of the cruise he turns up as Guido – black hat, overcoat and all on a beautiful Florida day. Jacques was dressed as a gangster's wife. The rest of us had spent the previous night organising because Marshall had to have all his audio and video equipment with him. We needed to hire three extra suites for all his shite. We also had to bring the team radios, as Marshall felt that communication was very important.

It wasn't too bad the first day. The ship was big enough to get lost in. We had dinner, went dancing. Then they shut the ship down at 11pm. Now what? That was just the first day. It went downhill from there: nothing worse than being stuck on a ship with a bunch of people with nothing to do all day but drink. Marshall got depressed and started calling us over the radios. We all took to hiding and when he called the radio you'd put your hand over the mike and make a lot of hissing and hacking sounds, like there was too much interference. Turns out our radios were illegal, as they interfered with the ship's navigation system. Just as I was doing an impression over the radio of the ship's Scottish captain, he walked up behind me and confiscated Marshall's entire communications network. I went to explain this to Marshall. He told me I was self-destructing.

Marshall and the First Lady weren't getting on too well. This wasn't so unusual. I was at his house in Detroit once when he was threatening to beat her up, causing such a disturbance that the police were called. There was a scuffle and Marshall grabbed the police officer's gun. He was arrested but instead of going to jail he was sent to the madhouse, where he recruited a couple of mechanics for the race team. He was out the next day after telling them he was a friend of Ronald Reagan's and was going to be President in 1992.

After one row, Jacques managed to get all his assets frozen. But he had to pay the guys on the team to keep it going. He had this limo – bulletproof, just like Reagan's – and he turned up at the workshop in it one day with its rear end virtually sitting on the ground. We opened the trunk and it was full of old paint cans. The cans were full of silver coins – and that's how he paid the guys that week. Then he and Jacques made up and all was back to 'normal'.

This time he threatened to throw her overboard and she was confined to the captain's quarters for her own protection for the remainder of the cruise. So she wasn't with us on the last night when Marshall entered us all in the ship's amateur singing contest. I baulked at this but instead of saying no volunteered to be the video guy. As I was watching I was struck by how sad it was that everybody was up doing something they didn't want to do – apart from Ricky, who won – just so they didn't 'self-destruct' and lose their livelihoods.

None of us could wait to get off that boat next morning. And no one wanted to keep him company on his chartered Lear back to Boca Raton; they all suddenly had somewhere else to be. I was the last one to be asked and because I wasn't ready to self-destruct, I accepted. I got all that audio/video shit back into the house there and the next day it was off to his place in Detroit, where I had to take the pictures off the wall and take them to his office downtown, up ten floors, and put them up there to hang for a couple of hours, then back again with them to the house, because he was suffering a depression and wanted to go home. All so I could be paid to drive a racing car.

This was my life now, and would be for a long time, just change the names and locations. This is what it had come to. That arrogant little fucker that was going to make it all happen had gone, drowned by what had happened since those cock of the walk days.

Emphasising how Tommy wasn't really on a career ladder, when he wasn't racing for the 'future president of the

USA' he was back in Formula Ford 1600, the junior racing category in which he'd been a double British champion six years earlier. But racing in America this time. It provided pocket money, confirmed Tommy as a gun for hire. He drove for a guy called Mike Gue and won all but one of the races contested, securing the South-East American championship.

When not racing for the future president or in Formula Ford, you might find him in an ARS car. These were single-seaters powered by Buick V6 engines and ARS was a feeder category into the premier American single-seater series, Indycar. It would become Tommy's bread and butter for the next few years. But it was while driving for Marshall Robbins in an IMSA race at Road Atlanta that Tommy met his future.

I'd qualified the Camaro fourth, but in the race I got hit from behind at the first turn and was T-boned. I continued but the car was falling apart and at the end of the race I just wanted to get the hell out of there. I was getting a lift from the team manager, my friend Mark Carbary. But he didn't want to head straight back to the hotel, he had to go to the infield to meet someone. I was complaining because all I wanted was a cool beer. We were driving a Camaro because Marshall insisted the whole team had Camaros – even though we weren't getting a penny from Chevrolet. Anyhow, coming the other way on the infield were two girls in another Camaro and they had beers. I told Mark to stop the car as I'd spotted my cool beer. We pulled them over, asked for a couple of beers. They obliged, I told them where we were staying and why didn't they stop by later and I'd repay them for the beers. I spent the next ten years paying for those beers! One of those girls was Shelly and just over a year later we got married.

Shelly was from Jacksonville, Florida, the daughter of Irene – a real southern lady with great poise, manners and hospitality – and Emory, a lawyer. Shelly was great fun, liked to party and was a great-looking girl. She'd been married before and was now divorced and had a cute five-year-old girl, Christy, who I came to love as my own.

I was living at the time at St Petersburg on the west coast of Florida, and the first time Shelly came to visit me there I got a call from her, saying her car had broken down. She'd been driving across a big bridge with the engine rattling and steam covering the windscreen. But she just kept right on, foot on the gas, until the thing died. She got it towed over to the other side of the bridge then called to tell me the good news. I picked her up and left the car there and a couple of days later I rented a Uhaul truck and a car trailer and towed it back. Cost me about $1,000 alltold. Later I moved into her place, which turned out to be Emory's place, which she was renting from him. Emory liked it when I moved in because the rent was now on time.

Irene and Emory were two of the nicest people you could meet. They actually seemed to like me – which was a real novelty as the parents of all my previous girlfriends never had done. Sometimes we'd all go out together and after a few drinks I'd start with the swearing and I'd hear Irene saying to Shelly, 'Is he saying what I think he's saying?' and Shelly would laugh and say, 'Yes Mom, I believe he is.'

CHAPTER TWELVE

An American Family

I didn't continue with the future president into 1987. I'd started doing ARS racing in '86, in between my commitments to Marshall Robbins. Kelly Agapiou, the guy I'd raced for in Formula Atlantic a couple of times in '83, had been put in charge of running a big fleet of these cars on behalf of the organisers, who were trying to get what was a new championship up and running. So Kelly had got me in to help set up the cars, get the fleet running properly, and in exchange I'd get to race there and earn some prize money. I'd jump from one car to another. With some help from a freelance, Gary Anderson, who was by now working for Galles – an Indycar team – I'd just get one car the way I liked it and after a couple of races it would be allocated to someone else coming into the series. So I'd have to start from scratch with another car. But that was OK, that was my role. In-between times I set a pole position and was getting good experience of the oval tracks. On top of that I'd gained in IMSA. It's a very different discipline to road racing, there's even less you can do as a driver to make a difference, and car set up becomes even more important. It was a whole new deal and I enjoyed learning it.

But for '87 Bill Boynton – the guy who I'd driven for in Super Vee and really hit it off with – was coming to ARS. He'd long been saying I was part of his plans and now he was as good as his word. I began winning races and setting poles and was involved in the fight for the championship with Didier Theys.

We came to Meadowlands, New Jersey, still in with a chance of the title. But I had something else to think about that weekend – I was marrying Shelly on the Monday after the race. Just about the whole wedding guest list was at the track cheering me on. The plan was to get married in a Manhattan registry office on Monday morning, then we were having the reception in the restaurant of a friend of mine, Eamonn Doran. He was also one of my sponsors, an Irish restaurateur I'd met when I was doing Formula Ford, who'd gone on to open this place in New York. As well as hosting the party, he was also organising the wedding. Although he gave me a good discount on renting his place I still had to pay him. It was three or four grand I simply didn't have. My plan was to win the race to earn enough prize money to pay Eamonn.

I qualified second to Theys, which was irritating. This guy had been kicking my ass most of the year, yet last time I raced him was in European F3 in '83, when he'd been nowhere. In fact, the only time I'd encountered him then was when I'd had an engine problem at Monza and everyone was passing me on the straights until I got so pissed off that the next guy who tried it, I put on the grass. That just happened to be Theys. Well, once the race got started it was Theys' turn to block me. He was running for the best team in the series at the time, Truesports, but this was a street course and I reckoned I could beat him anyway. But coming into the last lap I still hadn't found a chink of daylight in his blocking, so it was time to make a move, now or never.

We came past the start/finish line to go into the last lap and out the corner of my eye I could see Bill with his stopwatch at the pits. He had this really flamboyant way of using that watch. He'd follow the car like a cop with a radar gun, then as it came closer to him and came past he'd hit the stop very dramatically with a big proud look on his face. We raced down to turn one with the wall on the inside and Theys on the outside. It was going to be a 50/50 pass but I was going for it, I was coming through. Theys saw me and began squeezing me into the wall. I decided to hit Theys rather than the wall. We touched wheels, I went sailing up over the top of Theys, taking out the third-place car of Steve Millen, who we'd been about to lap. I landed heavily, like a baby giraffe trying to stand for the first time – right in front of the wedding party. Unfortunately, Theys' car was undamaged and he managed to get going and win the race. Now I'd no money to pay for the wedding. But if it had just been about the money I could've taken the second place and got five or six grand. Bill was fine about it all, saying he hired me to win races, not finish second.

By the time I got changed and joined the wedding party at turn one, things were pretty wild. Eamonn was locked in the toilet of the motorhome with his trousers around his ankles. One of his lady friends had fallen off the roof of the motorhome and received attention at the medical centre. Eventually we got Eamonn out of the toilet and got him home tucked up in bed. Me, Calvin Fish, David Kennedy and a few others headed off for a bachelor party and the girls got together and went off for a party of their own. At about midnight Eamonn rejoined us, having got out of bed. I asked him if everything was OK for tomorrow and he just started laughing, then fell over. Which made me kinda nervous.

Next morning we were up bright and early. We headed off to the registry office, which was right next to the Twin Towers. I was with Shelly, my friend Stuart Dent, Christy – who is Shelly's daughter – and Shelly's parents, Irene and Emory. We were waiting for Eamonn and the limo. And waiting and waiting. I looked at Irene and Emory, who like everything to be perfect, and there was definitely a bit of tension going on. Eventually, an hour late, here came Eamonn, still laughing. He went to the desk to get the info about where to meet the judge and my stomach dropped when I saw he was clearly getting into a heated discussion with her. Shelly glanced at her mother, her mother glanced at Emory, Emory glanced at me – and I looked at the pavement.

Eamonn returned and said there were no judges available because it was vacation time and they were all in the Hamptons. Emory saved the day. He was a lawyer from Jacksonville and he started flagging down other lawyers as they came out the courthouse.

Eventually, one of them put us in touch with a judge who would marry us. Then it was off to Eamonn's for his speciality: Irish Racing Lamb Chops. It was a great day and everyone partied into the night. We had a few days' honeymoon and then it was down to Pocono for the next race. This time I won – so I was able to pay Eamonn for the wedding.

Shelly was actually pregnant when we married. We hadn't planned it that way but we'd already decided we did want kids. Tommy Junior (T.J.) came along four months early. Shelly was already in hospital and began bleeding badly. I got a call from Irene at 2am. She told me they were going to take the baby now and that I should get to the hospital ASAP. I threw a couple of pillows in the back of the car and lifted Christy in there, still asleep. Emory and Irene lived about fifteen minutes away and I was about 40 minutes away. But, to their amazement, I arrived at the hospital the same time as them. T.J. weighed 4 pounds 3 ounces at birth. He was in good shape, but the next morning he took a turn for the worse when his right lung collapsed. They fixed that, then his left lung collapsed, they fixed that, then he had to have about three blood transfusions. It was touch-and-go for a while but he and Shelly both pulled through.

We then bought some land in Crescent City, a little town north-west of Daytona Beach. It was on a lake and had eight acres of scrubland and bush around it, which I intended to clear. I put a little modular home on there and that's where we lived. The idea was, when I made my millions, I'd move the modular house to the back of the property as a guest house and build our dream house where the modular house was. For the next seven years, in-between races, I cleared more of that scrub. In-between me clearing the scrub and racing the cars, another boy, Taylor, was born 10 September 1990.

Although my parents hadn't been able to make it out for the wedding, I did get to see them quite a lot between '87 and '92, thanks to the generosity of Bill Boynton. They would come over and stay for maybe a couple of months at a time for the next couple of years, until they could no longer travel because of their health. But at least I felt I'd been able to go some way to paying them back for getting me started and the money that I'd never paid back.

They were there at the end of '87 at the final ARS race. I ended up second in the championship, just a couple of points behind Theys. Close, but no cigar, yet considering it was a new team up against Truesports, we did OK. I knew that I was not moving up to Indycars because I didn't have the money to pay and there were no Indycar teams knocking on my door. I figured out who was driving for who, and who was looking, and who was not looking: so I didn't bother to call anybody, which was a trait of mine. I always figured if you were quick and won a lot of races, eventually somebody will notice and give you a chance. But this was America, where talent doesn't count the way it does in Europe, and I was getting older and I never begged for a drive in my life and I was not going to start now. I was getting paid a salary, so I was happy. I was still not looking to tomorrow, but I was spending money like I always did because I knew that I was still going to get the big drive and the million dollars some day – it was just a matter of time. But little did I know that time was running out.

After the Laguna race Bill threw a big banquet at the hotel. Afterwards, my Mam and Dad went to bed and Bill invited me, Shelly and my pal Stuart up to their suite for some more drinks. Mike Hooper – the guy who had been driving for Bill in Super Vee but who hadn't been up to it – was there too. Bill hadn't wanted to just cast him out so made him 'team coordinator', little more than a gofer really. But he still thought there was a chance he'd get rehired as a driver. I always felt there was more than a little jealousy from Mike towards me – understandable I guess, as Mike had been the guy that had brought Bill back into racing.

After a few drinks Bill fell asleep in his chair and Shelly, Stuart and I left and went to bed, but the party was still going on and Hooper was still there. Shelly said he'd made an inappropriate remark to her, something about how he'd like to give her another baby. I'd speak to him the next day about it. About an hour later I got a call and it was Susie, Bill's wife, possibly a bit worse for drink, just as we all were. She was saying why didn't we come back up. I asked if Hooper was still there and she said he wasn't, so I thought it was a great idea to go back, even though Shelly didn't. So I woke Stuart up and we went back up there. First person we saw as we got in the door was Hooper. And he's sitting next to Susie, getting way too friendly, and Bill's still asleep in his chair. So Stuart poured a glass of water over Hooper's crotch. 'What the fuck you doing?' shouts Hooper and Stuart said, 'Well, it looked like you needed cooling down.' And so a fight kicked off and I got involved too.

At which point, Bill wakes up and roars: 'Get out you bunch of heathens. I will not have fighting in my room. Get out.' We tried to explain but he was having none of it and as we went to the door Hooper muttered something about Shelly and I ran towards him from the bed I was standing on, launched myself through the air and punched him hard in the face as I was still flying through the air. It was a lucky but beautifully timed punch. 'Tommy, you're fired,' shouted Bill. As Stuart and I left, I replied: 'You can stick your drive up your arse.' Here was I, behaving like the knacker I am. The drink's a terrible curse.

Stuart and I then waited outside Hooper's room and when he came back we started laying into him again. This was all happening outside the room next to my Mam and Dad and next thing there's Mama at the door shouting at me, 'Thomas, stop that at once. You're losing your head!' Then she saw who it was we were fighting and said 'Oh, it's him is it?' Then she started kicking him too! She'd taken a dislike to him earlier in the evening, when she'd overheard him giving shit to some girls. The sight of my mother joining in was so funny that Stuart became helpless with laughter. Anyway, it all broke up and Shelly wouldn't allow me back in the room. I had to sleep on the floor of Mam and Dad's room.

Later, Bill unfired me and Hooper was fired, although I don't know if Bill ever realised how that fight started. We stayed together into '88 and won a few more races, but Bill was struggling with his health and finances and pulled out. Eventually he got a guy to run it for him but it meant I missed two races and in the end I just lost out in the title race once again, this time to Jon Beekhuis. There was something about Beekhuis I just didn't like and I didn't respect him as a driver, but I became really friendly with the guys that ran the team he drove for, Pig Racing, and a couple of years later I drove for them. At the '88 final in Miami I was leading the race, with Beekhuis in second, but that wasn't going to be enough for me to take the title. So I began to slow down, trying to get Beekhuis to try a pass on me so that I could then take him out. But the Pig Racing guys were onto what I was doing and told him on the radio not to try to pass me.

Anyway, Bill wasn't going to run a team in '89 so I was out of a drive and out of money. Then I got a call from a friend Gerry Maguire. He was a Belfast guy living in Canada and when I was racing in Pocono in '87 he'd come over to my trailer and introduced himself. We hit it off and became good friends. At Christmas '88 he'd read in a Toronto newspaper that a new team was being founded out of Toronto called Landford Racing. It was the project of a Canadian property developer and hobby racer, Tom Christoff. They were going to contest the '89 Indy Lights series (the new name for ARS) with Christoff as the driver. They were testing down at Sebring and Gerry suggested he call them on my behalf and offer my services as a driving coach. I had nothing else, so what the hell. Gerry did the deal and I showed up at Sebring. Tom wasn't there at first so I tested the car and got it to where it needed to be in terms of set up. Tom then showed up, a really big guy with flame-red hair. He wasn't very fast, I don't think he'd done much previous racing, but he had big balls. He would try to take 40mph corners at 140mph, which, as anyone in racing will tell you, doesn't work. Anyway, the guy running it for Christoff was Brian Stewart, a former racer, an aggressive character and a natural winner. I got the feeling he wasn't looking forward to messing around near the back so I mentioned that Bill Boynton still had my car from the previous year and I could probably get him to loan it to us. Brian talked Christoff into having a team-mate because it would be easier to get sponsorship if the team was a winning enterprise. I agreed to let Gerry be my manager and he did my deal and we won the first race, at Long Beach.

The following week Gerry went to the Toronto offices to collect my cheque. But Christoff took off about a third for Canadian taxes. But I wasn't living in Canada, and that wasn't the deal we'd agreed. Anyhow, Gerry got it fixed after a lot of discussion. But for the rest of the year Gerry would have to go to the office to get my cheque and every time they'd keep him waiting. It was difficult getting money out of the team and I think they were having some financial difficulties.

But on-track we had a really strong year. I was on pole for six of the twelve races and won four. Tom struggled a bit but you couldn't fault his bravery. We had two radios in each car, one to talk to the pits, one to talk to each other. This was so I could instruct him when we were out on track in practice. Then I'd get in front of him to show him the lines. But there was one race where I was leading but under big pressure from Paul Tracy and Juan Fangio III. We were coming to lap Tom and I thought, 'Good, he'll be able to help me.' No such luck. Instead, he decided he'd race me – despite being a lap down. He was slow through the corners but one thing he could do well was brake really late – so he was really hard to pass. I was scream-ing on the radio for him to get the fuck out the way, then the team were screaming at him. But it made no difference, he loved the limelight and here he was getting all of it. I found my own way by – eventually.

For the third consecutive year I went into the last round with a chance of taking the title. And for the third straight year I lost out, even though I'd now won more ARS/Indy Lights races than any other driver. My main rival for the '89 title was a guy called Mike Groff. The final round was again at Laguna Seca, a road course I felt was in my favour, as Groff was more of an oval track specialist. He was a couple of points ahead of me going in. Normally he'd always qualify in the first couple of rows but at this race there were quite a few road-racing guys having one-off events – people like P.J. Jones – and I figured the more of those guys that could get between me and Groff, the better my chances were. So anyone I figured might be able to beat him I approached and gave them my set up data to copy. It worked a treat. I set pole but Groff was way back in eighth. Perfect.

And so I set off in the lead, pulled it out to about five seconds and then just paced myself to the guy behind. It was all going beautifully. With three laps to go I was coming round a left-hand corner and I saw a backmarker up ahead spinning. He sort of half-caught it, then began spinning the other way, before pulling over to the left of the track and slowing right down. I was just changing up to fourth gear as I was passing him and he suddenly turned sharp right in front of me. We collided and the guy in second passed me but my car was still running. There was only one front wing and the other one was bent but I was still in second place, with Groff back in fifth. P.J. Jones was catching me and so I had to resort to some very defensive driving, blocking to keep him behind. Then the fourth-place car was behind us, then Groff was right there too, all in a big traffic jam behind me. I was holding them up by about five seconds per lap, braking early, trying to make it so chaotic behind me that someone would collide with Groff. I managed to hold them back for two laps but then ran wide and a couple of cars came past, one of them being Groff. So there went my championship.

Actually I wasn't too upset. Had I won the title my share of the prize money would've been around $80,000 – but I wasn't sure I'd get paid. This way I didn't need to worry about it.

Afterwards there was a big party in town at Fisherman's Wharf, a restaurant owned by my friends, Jo and Cathy. It was kind of a tradition that we went there whenever we raced in Laguna. I was running a little late and when I got there the place was overflowing with people. Jo shouted me to come into the kitchen to help and I asked how come it was so crazily busy? And she said: 'Don't ask me. They're your friends!' Seems like I'd invited a few more people than I'd realised and they, in turn, had invited another five or six people each. At the end they had to lock the doors and anyone that tried to get in Jo would get me to OK them first. Well, I was sitting down and someone shouted, 'Tommy can these guys come in?' and I looked outside, and who was there but Tyler Alexander, the guy that had run my ill-fated McLaren test all those years ago. So I told Jo not to let him in. Tyler wouldn't have even known who the party was for, but it gave me great pleasure to keep him out. After all, to my mind he'd played his part in keeping me out of F1.

The original plan for Tom and his team had been to

launch in Indycars after the season of Indy Lights. After a few Indy Lights races Tom asked me to be one of the drivers for the 1990 Indycar team. We agreed terms and shook on it but a contract was never drawn up. He got as far as buying a used Indycar chassis, but as the season went on I became more certain that the funds weren't there to make it happen. A lot of bills were going unpaid and people were getting upset. Eventually the Indycar deal was knocked on the head and that was actually quite a blow for me. It was the first time I seriously began to think there might not be a million-dollar deal just down the road, that I might be struggling on the margins forever.

I had nothing going into the 1990 season. Landford were continuing but they needed a driver with a budget so they took Paul Tracy, a quick but accident-prone guy who had spent the last couple of years in Indy Lights – crashing. But his father was backing his career. Just to keep the money coming in I began working at race schools, doing ride and drive days, where you'd instruct pupils in a road car, then let them take you around. My friend Calvin Fish was doing this already and he helped get me the gig.

Part-way through the season an Indy Lights team, Genoa Racing, got in touch with me. Their driver had clashing commitments in five of the Indy Lights races and they invited me to be the stand-in. Paul Tracy was dominating the series for my old team – and I could understand how. He was a quick guy, but more importantly, he was joining a team with a very bright, up-and-coming engineer, Burke Harrison. By contrast, my engineer at Genoa was one of the most difficult guys I've ever worked with. Even though I was the winningest driver in the history of the championship, he would not listen to a word I said, and it was a constant shit-fight trying to make changes to the car. The only thing worse than his attitude was his wig: so I wasn't getting too many good results. But it came good in my final race with them, at Detroit.

I qualified third, which was a bit of a struggle, and in the race I was running second to Tracy, but he was disappearing up the road at about one second per lap. I was content; this was the best this car could do and I was on 50 per cent of the prize money. But then, late in the race, there was a full-course yellow – which meant I could get myself right back on Tracy's ass. Suddenly the game was on. They were trying out a new start system, where the cars ran two-by-two under the yellow period instead of in a long line. Perfect. After a while they gave us the sign that the green flag would come at the end of the next lap, and racing would be back on. So part-way through the last yellow flag lap, I took off and entered the main straight with a huge lead over Tracy – which they were never going to allow so the guy had to throw the yellow again, giving us an extra caution lap. It was risky because they might have penalised me for not being in position, but it did two things: it reduced by a lap the number of racing laps I'd have to try to keep a faster car behind me – assuming I could get the lead – and it also screwed with Tracy's head. So now, as we're back in the correct order on the new yellow flag lap, I radioed in and asked my crew chief what flags has the starter got in his hands? He told me he had the white in one hand and the green in the other. I asked where's the yellow? Behind him. OK, keep an eye on that yellow, I told him. As we're getting to the last straight I asked again, where's the yellow? Still behind him. So I knew he was going to throw the green, there wasn't enough time to pick up the yellow – so I made a break for it, past Tracy, right under the starter's nose. Know your competition! And I knew Paul.

I led him through turn one and then hugged the right of the track for the next right-hander – no way was he coming down my inside. And I was determined he wasn't going to go around the outside either. I'd decided it was shit or bust, I'd rather crash than lose the lead. If I wasn't going to win, neither was he. But as it turned out I didn't need to resort to that – he crashed into the wall all on his own coming out of turn two. After the race everyone who'd forgotten me was there shaking my hand, buying me drinks. I was briefly The Man again. My share of the purse was $15,000 and Angelo, the team owner – who was a real gent – paid me that night. Little did I know it, but it was the last race I'd ever win in America.

The gunslinger had just won his last race in America. It had been a good four-year run. With a tiny bit of luck and a following wind Tommy would have been ARS/Indy Lights champion for three consecutive years: 1987, '88 and '89. Would it have made any difference? Probably not. He was unique in being a paid professional in a series otherwise populated by young up-and-comers trying to make a name for themselves. They were paying, Tommy was being paid. Guys like Paul Tracy were paying to enhance their future prospects. Tommy's prospects were in the past and his reluctance to go chasing drives or sponsors – the idea of which he found demeaning – just ensured there was no big-time career in America waiting for him, just as there hadn't been in Europe. Having someone of Tommy's calibre in Indy Lights made it more difficult for those young guys to make their reputations, but even in his directionless late-80s spec rather than his lean, hungry early-80s incarnation, he still made for a great measuring stick. The talent was still intact even if the application, ambition, hunger, direction – whatever you might call that drive that gives you a goal and makes you push towards it – was long gone. It was sad that such a devastating talent was eking out a living in a sideshow. Now, even that was coming to an end.

CHAPTER THIRTEEN

The Rock Star And The Undercover Cop

For 1991 I did an Indy Lights deal with Pig Racing. It was called that because it belonged to Norm Turley, and he and his family were all cops from Long Beach, California. I'd been racing against them for four years and had got to know them really well. As well as Norm there was his father John, his brother Walt, and their friends Tim Bonney and Daddyo. Cops, all of 'em. The Pig guys had always wanted me to drive for them but it could never happen because they didn't have the budget. But for '91 they'd done a deal to run the rock star Vince Neal from Motley Crew. The band had kicked him out because he was spending so much time racing and not enough in the studio. Vince was paying Pig to run him so suddenly they had a budget and were able to run a second car for me alongside Vince, the idea being I could also be Vince's driving coach.

As you'd expect, Vince was a wild character. He lived in LA and we'd go testing in Phoenix. He'd helicopter in and helicopter back out again at the end of the day because his wife Sherice didn't trust him to spend the night in case he went off with some women or got drunk when he was supposed to be on the wagon. He was actually a pretty good driver with good car control, especially when he hadn't got drunk the night before. Vince's assistant actually looked a lot like Vince and whenever the girls yelled 'Vince' at him, he'd answer and was only too pleased to take advantage of the mistaken identity. He'd a constant supply of blow jobs. As did Vince. He'd be walking back to the trailer and a girl would just come up to him and ten minutes later he'd come out the trailer with a smile on his face and then his guy would come looking for him and ferry him back to Sherice, who'd got to wondering where he'd gone. One time, after a race at Long Beach, we were in a bar and he took me aside, thanked me for all my help and slipped me a big wad of cash. I counted it later and it was $1,000.

But on track things weren't going too well. They were trying to run an Indycar as well as the two Indy Lights and the money was just stretched too tight. Norm was really scrimping to try to make it work, and I later found out he'd even hocked his home to keep going. Like a lot of people in racing he'd become consumed by it and it wiped him out financially. At one race my car was so bad I was lapped. When Vince then lapped me I decided I'd had it. Especially when Norm didn't seem too interested. My American career had definitely petered out but I did enjoy being with those guys.

Norm's brother Walt took me along on rides when he was working at Long Beach. He told his superintendent that I was an undercover cop from Ireland, come to see how they did things over here. We went on undercover stings all over the city. Once we got a call saying a guy was selling crack outside a school, so we drove round there in our undercover Camaro, parked round the corner and waited. Next thing I knew Norm came tearing up beside the guy. Walt threw me a gun, said 'Cover me,' and jumped out. As Norm grabbed him the guy tried to swallow the crack and Walt was there with his hand down the guy's throat retrieving the evidence.

So the guy pretending to be a racing driver but who was really a rock star had lapped the guy who really was a racing driver but had been pretending to be a cop! Got that?

Another day we staked out a store all day, waiting for a suspected robber who'd been seen going in there to come back out. We were there until 6pm before the guy came out – turns out he was working there! Other times we'd stake out bars where parole guys hung out. One of the cops was disguised as a drunk bum, sleeping outside the door of the bar with his social security cheque and some dollars hanging out of his pocket. You'd see these guys come out the bar, walk past and do a double take, but the first few didn't take the bait. Finally, one guy comes out, looks, walks past, and you can see him thinking as he's walking down the road, wondering whether he should turn back and take the money. We're watching this from inside a van with two-way windows and curtains and a periscope like on a submarine. Walt's watching through it, saying, 'Oh yeah, he can smell it, go on baby go back and get it, a lot of money there, a lot of money to buy crack, you know you want it, you know you love that crack.' And it's getting very hot and smelly in that van with three big Long Beach cops and one Irish 'cop'-cum-racing driver. Eventually the guy decided to go for it and walked up to the 'bum', grabbed everything that was sticking out his pocket and ran. Walt shouted into the radio, 'He's taken the bait, go, go, go!' and all these cops descended on the guy, cuffed him and put him in a wagon. There was lots of cheering and high-fiving, it was quite a thrill.

Yes, it was entrapment. But there was a bigger picture. A couple of weeks earlier a family had been murdered in their home, bullets to the back of their heads, execution-style. The police needed leads and the idea was to get these paroles into trouble. As paroles they knew they could be going straight back to jail: so instead of that, they might trade any information they knew about the murders.

It was a fascinating glimpse of a different sort of world. Meantime, my own world was beginning to fall apart.

CHAPTER FOURTEEN

Down, Down Mexico Way

In between drives I was getting by with my ride and drive days at various racetracks. I also did some commentating for ESPN on the South American F3 races in '91 and '92. Confirming my suspicions that the million-dollar deal might never happen, I was working with a whole lot of refugee racers, guys who were struggling to stay in the game, good drivers too: Calvin Fish, John Paul Jr, Robby and Johnny Unser and SCCA sports car drivers still trying to make it – guys like Randy Pobst and Terry Borscheller. There was a big bunch of egos together in the same place at the race school, all with their own sorry tales of woe. Don't get me wrong, I enjoyed the instruction, really liked communicating with the pupils, had a great laugh and made a lot of friends. But in the back of my head, the clock was ticking down, my debts were going up and my marriage was on the rocks.

I was running out of ideas. Things had got so bad going into '93 I had the idea of selling one of my helmets just to get some money. I was supplied a certain number free each year from Bell, so I phoned my old buddy from Formula Ford days, Alfonso Toledano, who was now back in Mexico, and asked if he could sell it there? He said why didn't I come down to Mexico myself – I might be able to get a drive? He told me the racing scene was thriving there, so I hopped on a plane the next weekend and headed for a race meeting in Mexico City. Alfie introduced me to a load of people, including his friend Orchio, who ended up buying my helmet for $1,500 – way overpriced.

Orchio then became my best friend. He said I'd saved his life by selling him the helmet – I could never see the logic of that, especially as he didn't race or even ride a motorbike! Whatever. Orchio was a rich playboy alcoholic manic-depressive bisexual. He could be a really nice guy but you never quite knew which Orchio you were going to get. I'd meet him in his office each morning and try to judge from his facial expressions which mood he was in. Trouble was the facial expressions changed by the second – happy, sad, mad, sad, happy ...

I hadn't known him long when he took me with his friend/servant Pepe out to a racetrack about four hours' drive out of Mexico City, in Nacho's Dodge Ram. I was half-asleep in the back and they were talking to each other in Spanish. We were out in the middle of nowhere and Orchio began looking back at me with his funny sad, mad, happy facial expressions. Then he would say something to Pepe and they'd both then look at me. Next thing I know, Orchio has a gun in his hand. Now I started to shit myself. I didn't really know these guys and I'm thinking I'm about to be shot – probably for ripping off Orchio with the helmet. I sat up and started talking twenty to the dozen, then Orchio motioned for Pepe to pass the car in front. 'Thank God,' I thought, 'they're not going to kill me, they're going to kill the people in the car.' Then I thought, 'Yeah, but then I'm a witness to a murder so they'll then kill me.' Suddenly Pepe passed the car and pulled away at about 100mph, leaving the car well behind in our dust and then when there was a quiet piece of road Pepe slowed, Orchio opened his window, looked at me one more time – then shot at a signpost and missed! So much for murder in Mexico! I'd been shitting myself for about half an hour. Over the coming months I came to realise that Orchio just liked playing with guns – and that he was a hopeless shot.

I picked up a drive in the Mexican F3 championship with Alberto Lozano. He had sponsorship from Corona and Quaker State but still didn't have quite enough money for the best kit. So I'd ask Alberto how much for a new engine, he'd tell me and I'd tell Orchio – who would then give Alberto the money. Over the next couple of years Orchio probably spent around $300,000 buying equipment for us.

Mexico was one big party, which, with my marriage breaking up back home, was good in one way. I could open my cell phone and call ten different people to go out to lunch. Lunch would lead to a club that night and home by 5am and there was always a lot of good weed to smoke. I'd been smoking this for the last ten years and was quite a connoisseur. They called it 'green of the grass' in Mexico. I would stay with my friend Brian Ireland, an Irish ex-racer who was now working as a race engineer out here, or with Pepe or with driver friends like Rogelio Rodriguez or Rod Macleod. I made a lot of good friends out there, who I'm still in touch with today.

But I had to be careful not to let Orchio know if I'd been partying without him. Because he'd get insanely jealous. He liked me – maybe a little too much! He told me he loved me. I told him I loved girls. If we'd had a good race, Orchio would hire a whole load of hookers for us to celebrate with. One time we were all in Orchio's office, everybody naked, and I'm bent over this girl. Next thing I know Orchio is trying to mount me! I'm trying to see to this girl at the same time as trying to swat Orchio off me. I was just starting to think what a funny scene this was when I looked over at Orchio's bodyguard and suddenly I felt a little scared because the guy always carried a gun and I didn't like or trust him.

Guns were a big thing in Mexico and I always thought they were a very bad idea, especially when there were so many drugs around too. One time I got off the plane and was looking for Pepe, who normally came to pick me up in Orchio's Dodge. No sign, so I called Orchio who said, 'Oh Pepe cannot make it, just get a cab to the office.' When I got there I asked where Pepe was and Orchio was very nervous/sad/happy/mad/pensive. Turned out Pepe had had a fight with his wife – and shot her. Luckily, he was an even worse shot than Orchio, so he hadn't killed her, but she was hurt. He'd driven her to the hospital, dumped her there and was now on the run. I felt bad for her and their two kids and visited her in hospital. We talked but then her brothers arrived looking for revenge. They knew I was a friend of Pepe's so I headed for the salida (the exit; I was picking up the lingo now), got a taxi and got the hell out of there. Pepe turned up later that week and eventually handed himself in. Orchio celebrated by hiring some hookers.

We had a few good races that year and I was fourth in the championship. I renewed my F3 deal with Alberto Lozano for '94. But there was another series for more powerful cars, F2. A Mexican former Indycar driver, Josela Garza, ran the Sección Amarilla (Yellow Pages) F2 team and his driver, Marco Magnia, was killed at Monterray when a piece of tarmac was lifted by the car in front of him and thrown into his helmet. So Josela needed a new driver and gave me a call. He had me test the car and I was quick, so we went to his motorhome to do a deal. I said I needed $5,000 per race plus expenses. He said that was more than he wanted to pay. I asked how much he was thinking of and he told me $1,000. I said I couldn't do it for that and we settled on $2,000 plus expenses – plus a full minibar in my hotel room, and when I landed in Mexico I wanted the cash in an envelope before I got in the car. Josela agreed and was as good as his word. Every time I got off the plane from America his guy would be there with an envelope of cash.

Allen Berg was the big star of Mexican F2. I knew him from my time in British F3 back in '82 when we'd raced together – well, he'd been in the same races as me but I didn't actually race him, he was nowhere near. In Mexico he was driving for Team Marlboro, the big team, and had been doing it a long time and was the big hotshot. In my first F2 race I qualified second to him and in the race I was running right on his ass, looking for a way past. There was a chicane and he was taking a wide line and with one lap to go I went for the inside. We collided and were both out. It was just a normal 50/50 racing incident but the local racing press went berserk. They were calling for my licence and saying I should never be allowed to race in Mexico again. There were conspiracy theorists saying I'd been brought over from F3 to make sure Marlboro didn't win the championship. The politics there were worse than in F1.

After qualifying second in my first race I never qualified better than fifteenth in my next four – as my engines had suddenly become pathetically under-powered. The F3 organisation then came and told me they didn't want me to drive for the rival F2 series any more. I told them I'd given Josela my word and I couldn't just back out of it, plus he was paying me $5,000 per race and I needed the money. I said they had to pay me what I would lose and to my astonishment they agreed to pay me $30,000 cash over three months. I told Josela what had happened and he understood, but he was never the same with me again. It was a great deal for me, especially as I'd been knobbled by my engines, in F2 anyway. It was the first time I'd ever been paid not to race.

So I just continued in F3 with Alberto Lozano and we finished third in the championship. It was a fantastic, fun place to be and I particularly enjoyed the 'green of the grass'. So much so, in fact, that I decided to smuggle some back to America. I had my golf clubs with me and I used to match up different grips with different heads, using a special torch. You'd heat up the head of the club and you'd be able to detach it from the shaft. Then to put it back on you'd just use special golf club glue. So the plan was to fill the shaft with as many joints as I could fit inside (ten, as it turned out). With it all sealed up and glued, hopefully the sniffer dogs at the airport wouldn't pick it up.

When the time came for my flight I was having second thoughts but went for it. I travelled to Orlando first class, so was feeling no pain by the time I arrived. I picked up my golf clubs very relaxed, walked out the airport and went home – success. Then I got my #3 titanium out the bag, heated up the head, slid it off and shook the club upside-down. Nothing came out. So I got out the hacksaw. After about five minutes of that I realised I was getting nowhere – you can't really saw through titanium. I was so pissed off that I then put the club over my knee and broke it in two, destroying a couple of the joints (as well as the club). All that for eight poxy joints. Looking back now, I just think: 'Why?'

It was while I was racing in Mexico that we heard Ayrton Senna had been killed in the Grand Prix. A lot of us in the paddock were interviewed on TV about it. I felt bad, but it wasn't like I'd lost a close friend. We'd had our differences in the past, when we were both trying to make our way, but that was ancient history. We'd long ago made up. There was the time when I helped get him drunk in Macau and a few years later when he'd left Lotus and gone to McLaren I asked if he could make me an introduction to the Lotus boss Peter Warr – which he did, and which he didn't have to do. It came to nothing, as Warr made it clear he had no interest in me, but I mention it just to illustrate that Ayrton and I were OK with each other. Other guys being interviewed were crying like they'd lost their closest buddy, yet none of these guys were even that close to Ayrton.

Great fun though Mexico was, it was all just a bit too insane. The last F3 race I won Orchio did his usual and hired a bevy of hookers to celebrate. He had four of them upstairs and I was keeping the other two company downstairs. Suddenly there were gunshots coming from upstairs and screaming. I opened the door and the four terrified hookers were running down the stairs, screaming for their lives, tits flying up and down. They hid in the office. I went upstairs and there was Orchio, naked, with a gun in each hand, waving them around, pissed off about something. I tried to talk to him but he shot at me. Luckily he was still a terrible shot and he missed, so I ran back downstairs and hid in the same room as the girls and locked the door. He was outside that door with his guns for about half an hour with me trying to talk sense into him. Eventually he agreed to put the guns down. I opened the door and the girls ran off. I spent a bit of time talking Orchio down and as soon as he wasn't watching I removed all the bullets from his guns. It was about 4am now – and he went to sleep.

At about 7am I was awoken by the sound of Orchio looking for his bullets. 'Now, why does he want his bullets?' I thought. That was my cue to get the fuck out of there. Out of Orchio's place – and out of Mexico. It was over.

Two weeks later Alberto Lozano phoned to tell me Orchio was dead. He had drowned in his swimming pool. He was not quite forty and left a boy not quite two. He also left around $40 million.

Things were pretty awful when I got back. Shelly

had finally dumped me. She had a new boyfriend and wanted me out the house. But why should I leave? I refused and so for a while we were still all living there, even though Shelly and I were no longer a couple. Eventually she and the kids moved out and I became a basket case. I had no drive, no money, I'd lost my family and my confidence – and I began drinking from the moment I got up till the moment I went to bed. I was the clichéd guy going through a divorce, phoning up his friends wanting to talk about it until eventually they just avoided me.

I decided I had to pick myself up somehow. Although I was still drunk or high most of the time, I got a job with a friend in Crescent, Scott, who had a few ferneries. I would clear land for him, fix his equipment – just labouring, basically. If I was mowing with a tractor I would always try to get right up to the edge so there wasn't as much to trim afterwards and often I'd end up breaking a water pipe or breaking the tractor. Once or twice I was mowing around his lake, got too close and slid in, then I'd have to get someone to tow me out. I blew three tractors like that, but I'd then fix them. I got into bulldozing in a big way. I felt like Superman being able to knock over a monster tree. I was doing this for about an hour once and had cleared a whole acre, then Scott arrived and told me I'd cleared the wrong bit of land! I just had no control over myself.

The job was just enough to pay Shelly the child support but the debts were mounting up. Late payments on the place were up to $55,000, though I'd already paid about $120,000. It was worth about $80,000, so I had to sell. Eventually, one of my friends and his wife took over the loan, sorted it out and moved in. I got

$1,000 cash, gave Shelly $800. Leaving me with $200 for seven years hard work. Now the place is probably worth around half a million.

Because most of my friends were avoiding me I started hanging around with a guy from work, Durant, an ignorant redneck. We'd hang around with his redneck friends and some Mexicans – and I fit right in. They'd cook food in their 50-gallon drums. Then, after they'd got enough beer and crack inside them (I never got so low that I joined them in taking crack) the guns would come out and they'd start shooting at things. In this state, Durant was as danger- ous as Orchio, and it would be time for me to leave. They'd also have cockfighting contests. T.J. and Taylor were starting to come over to stay with me by this time and they bugged the shit out of me to get them a fighting cock of their own. We got one and tied it to a tree. T.J. told one of the teachers at school and I had to deny it because they are illegal.

Before I'd moved out of the house by the lake, I told Durant one day that he could come to my house any- time, use the lake and that he could bring his sister and her kids. A few days later I heard a truck coming down the drive. I looked out and there was Durant in his truck with about six more trucks behind him with about twenty rednecks aboard. I locked all the doors and hid in my room. Durant came up banging on the door: 'Come on Tommy you fucker, we know you're in there!' I had to hide in my house for the next five hours until they left.

Durant was OK until he got some drink or crack into him, but next time I saw him after he'd turned up at the house, he was pissed. I was in a bar with my buddy Stuart, who was visiting from England. Durant wandered over to our table and started giving us shit. He was going to kick our asses. He looked at me and said he was going to kick my ass. I then confused him by asking if there was any particular reason he was going to kick my ass and he started stammering, confused. Eventually he was thrown out and Stuart and I looked at each other and laughed. Just another day in Crescent City. I'd once been the hotshot racing driver in town, now I was just a washed-up fuck-up that fitted right in among the hill-billies. I was the knacker from Dundalk.

My good friends Maurice and Rose, from Ireland, came to visit me around this time. I remember I'd just got in from work on the tractor and was covered in grime and we were playing pool. Rose said she'd never seen me looking so bad. I laughed and said 'I know' because I just didn't care. It was the lowest point of my life.

It was thirteen years since Ayrton Senna and Tommy Byrne, the two outstanding future F1 prospects of their generation, had stood arguing in the Van Diemen offices. One of them was now in his grave, deified like no driver ever has been. The other was a depressed, drunk, labourer.

It was my friend Calvin Fish who pulled me out of my depression. He was working as a race driving instructor at the Mid Ohio circuit. He talked the chief instructor, another ex-racer called Chris Kniefel, into hiring me. That's when I started to get back on my feet and I'm still working there today. Calvin has been a really good friend for over 25 years and has always stuck by me – which is quite something from another driver. He's a class act.

CHAPTER FIFTEEN

Letting Go

Getting stuck into work at Mid Ohio and getting my personal life straight – and seeing my boys – brought some meaning into my life in the aftermath of those desperate times, when I was heading nowhere fast and drunk. I might not ever be in line to make the millions I'd once thought were coming my way, but I was at least now functioning properly. I guess with age had come acceptance.

I got together with Michele, a girl I'd known before I married Shelly. In the meantime she'd been through a failed marriage too. She's a very organised, disciplined person and probably just what I needed. T.J. and Taylor came to spend more time with us and she was able to give them a structure that I'd not been able to. Then we had a child together, a boy, Cullen, who was born on 7 July 1999.

When not at our place in Florida I would travel to Mid Ohio, which is several hundred miles away, and decamp there while the instruction courses were going on. I came to enjoy my time there and still do. And when I hear about the dreams and hopes of young drivers and their families I try not to dwell on what might be ahead of them, I try not to remember my own experiences, the hard work and where it all led. I just tell them where to brake, shift, turn the wheel, when to get on the gas, try to feel the car, try to be smooth.

It's a living and I enjoy it, even though it's the nearest I've ever had to a nine-to-five. But in 2002 it led me to a strange place – another one! It all started when my friend and fellow instructor Tony Kester asked if I could coach this guy Richard Millman because he had too much on. I was always looking for more work and agreed. Tony said that the guy was slow but listened well and had plenty of money. He was about to start racing in the Ferrari Challenge, a series for road-going Ferrari 360s. When the guy turned up I couldn't even understand how he fitted into a Ferrari 360 – he must've weighed 350 pounds. His first race was at Lime Rock and I turned up there to see how he got on. When you're coaching guys at this stage, they need more than just a coach, you end up being their assistant: Where do I sign in? How do I get out of the pits? Do you think I've time to go to the shitter before I get in the car? Yeah, you've plenty of time, go to the shitter. No, I don't think I do have time. What time are we on track? The same time as last time you asked five minutes ago you fat dumb fuck (thought, not said). And he was a diabolically bad driver. But he had a trained brain ... That's what he told me: 'Tommy, you need only tell me anything once. Because I have a trained brain.' OK, whatever.

All this would've been OK if he'd been a nice guy. But he was an asshole, always screaming and shouting at everyone, barking his orders. I'd come full circle in 25 years: working for Fat Bastard was almost like working for Crawford again. You're thinking why didn't I just tell him where to shove it, aren't you? Well, he was paying a thousand bucks a day, he had booked me for 100 days and I had a wife and three kids to provide for ...

After that first race I did a coaching session with him at Summit Point. His race car blew its engine quite early in the day but he'd driven there in his road-going model, so he had them put the slick tyres on that, just so I could instruct him. I drove first, with him alongside me. I was showing him the lines, telling him where to brake and turn, just the very basic stuff. Then we swapped over. On the first lap, going through the fastest turn on the track, he just somehow forgot to turn the steering wheel. As he realises he's running out of road, he puts the steering on in a big hurry and of course that upsets the car and now we're spinning onto the grass. The grass was damp and so the car actually accelerated – right into a tree, on its side. We were up the trunk at an angle of about 45 degrees. As the dust settled I looked across at Millman and he was hanging in his belts and his eyes were rolling around in his head. 'Oh great, he's fucking dead on the first day!' I thought to myself. Then, as I went to help him he came to – and immediately he starts trying to get the car started, like he's trying to run off from the scene or something. I'm shouting at him: 'Richard!

You are stuck on a tree. Switch it off.' Eventually he took in the situation. But it was about five minutes before anyone noticed we were missing and came to look for us.

They had to get a chainsaw to separate the car from the tree. My ribs were hurting like hell because I'd cracked a couple of them. But amazingly the car's suspension turned out to be straight and he went back out in it later in the day. I asked him what had happened at that turn and he replied, 'I was just doing the same as you!' This was to become standard procedure. Every time the fucker crashed, he blamed me.

Millman had a girlfriend, Kathleen, an Irish-Korean and an aspiring musician. She'd met him at a Ferrari track day. They looked the oddest couple – because she was tiny, weighing less than 90 pounds – which was about 260 pounds lighter than him. He treated her like shit, always putting her down.

I eventually hooked him up with a guy called Leo Hendrie, an entrepreneur who would take an ailing company, fix it up and sell it on for a big profit. He was a very smart guy and I'd met him when I was instructing at Mid Ohio. We hit it off great and he'd begun to help me finance my son T.J.'s kart racing. Leo was racing in the Porsche GT Rolex series, a one-make championship for GT3 911 Porsches. He had a friend also entering a car who needed a paying driver. Millman looked up to Leo so it wasn't too hard putting together a deal that saw me sharing a Porsche with Fat Bastard. Cost him about $1.3 million.

The first race was at Homestead and the night before I was with Millman at the hotel with my friend Tony when Kathleen turned up, about 11.30. Millman didn't say anything to her but just took himself off to his room. Kathleen stayed for about fifteen minutes chatting with Tony and me. Then we all retired to our rooms. About 6am I was woken by a ringing phone. I picked up the receiver: 'Is Kathleen with you?' barked Millman.

'What? No, she's not Richard. Why?'

'Have you spoken to her this morning?'

'No, I haven't seen her since last night downstairs. Why?'

'Meet me downstairs, now,' he ordered.

So I walked down to the lobby and there was Kathleen already sitting there. I told her Fat Bastard was looking for her. She said they'd had a row and she'd got another room. Then he turned up and saw us there together and began screaming and shouting. 'I know where you were last night, you whore – you were with Tommy. Tommy, you better fuck off and work for Leo.' So I'd apparently lost my job before I'd even started. For something I hadn't done. I didn't even fancy her!

But it blew over and I raced the Porsches with him for a while. We weren't given the same engines as the favoured guys, plus I had the handicap of him, so we never figured. But that wasn't what finished us off. It was a weekend in 2003 when he decided to take his classic Ferrari 275 to the Le Mans historic meeting. He'd asked me to share the driving with him, which I was happy to do, as I was going to be there coaching him anyhow.

Before travelling to Le Mans we stopped off at Paris, at a very expensive hotel Millman always stayed at when he was here. It was amazing watching all the staff lick his ass and I could see why he liked coming here. It gave him the illusion of respect. Although I called him Richard, in my mind he was simply 'Fat Bastard' and I referred to him as that when I talked about him to Kathleen.

I didn't fancy hanging around listening to these people licking his ass all night so I slipped off and found an English-style pub. I was sitting there minding my own business and this English guy with tattoos all over his arms came over and began talking. He was tall and muscle-bound, looked like a mean bastard, and was half-shitfaced. Turns out he was an ex-SAS soldier and had served in Northern Ireland where some of his friends had been killed. At first he was my friend and got me talking about 'The Troubles' and asking me why the English were even over there in the first place. I agreed with him – and at that point he turned. 'I'll tell you why we were there,' he says. 'To kill Irish fucks like you.' His eyes were watering with rage and hatred and I was shitting myself. Why the fuck couldn't I just get out for a quiet drink? 'Yes, yes, they were your friends,' I babbled, 'and that was a terrible thing that happened,' really licking ass to try to save mine.

'Well, now I'm really going to fuck you up you little Irish bastard,' he says as I'm eying which door I can run for. Then he started laughing his head off. 'Tommy boy, I'm just messing with you. I'm half-Irish myself. Let's have another drink.' Now he's slobbering all over me. The last thing I wanted to do was have a drink with him, but I was scared. He tortured me for the next two hours until eventually he got up to go to the pisser and I was out of there like a shot.

I ran back to the hotel and what's confronting me as soon as I enter the lobby? Millman and Kathleen rowing at the top of their voices. Three hundred and fifty pounds and six chins of sweaty anger clocks me and says: 'She says you call me Fat Bastard!' Oh shit, could tonight get any worse? It was just the beginning of a week from hell with Fat Bastard.

As part of the weekend there was a very fancy do at a castle near Le Mans, and the three of us turned up there. There was a table plan but that didn't stop Millman from demanding to be seated at a different table, he was so arrogant. Kathleen and I were almost dying from embarrassment. The waiter very politely told him it wasn't his table and that he would escort him to his and Millman went berserk, screaming like a madman. Making it even more embarrassing for me was the fact that the guest of honour was Jacques Laffite, the French ex-F1 driver who had been one of the stars when I'd driven the Theodore. The last time I'd seen him he was bawling me out – very charmingly – for getting in his way on the track in '82. Now, here he was, watching me cringe while this lunatic I was babysitting made an ass of himself. Later, after a few drinks, I went over to Laffite, reintroduced myself and reminded him of what he'd said all those years ago. He's a lovely man and we got to chatting for quite a while. Millman hated me diverting attention from him and became even more obnoxious for the rest of the night.

I'd had it with him, but it all finally came to a head a few weeks later at a race at Phoenix. I'd done the first stint in the car and I handed it over Millman. He went out and coasted through the first couple of turns at about 40mph like there was no one else on the track. The leaders were approaching him flat out and he nearly took James Weaver off. The organisers went nuts and black-flagged him. He came in and stormed off while I took over again, now many laps down. He was always being black-flagged, he was around 25 seconds off the pace so was a hazard. The team manager was always having to invent different excuses as to why it kept happening, because the guy would just not accept that he was a wanker driver. I knew when he stormed off that was the end, and I was relieved. He went off and did a deal to run with another fat bastard. I figured at least the car's corner weights could now be the same! That deal ended up with people suing each other.

But Millman wasn't quite the end for me. A team owner called Chuck Goldsborough was. One of my instructor friends, Ian James, drove for him and Ian was always asking me to join him there. Whenever I asked how much Goldsborough would pay, the answer was always that he wanted me to drive for free. It was a matter of pride to me that I'd always been paid to drive. We still hadn't agreed a deal but he entered me for a race in his fourth car – a Lexus Estate – alongside Johnny Rutherford IV, another instructor friend and a good guy. Johnny said, 'Please Tommy, it's only for one stint' and I still refused. About two hours before the race Goldsborough came across. I told him I wanted $2,000 to drive. He said he couldn't pay that. 'Tommy, think of all the exposure you'll get driving for Team Lexus,' he said. 'Fuck the exposure,' I told him, 'I need to get paid.' Eventually we did a deal. I was helping a young racer, Tim Barber – a quick young guy who could drive anything fast – and I told Goldsborough that if he put Tim in the car for free at the next race, I'd drive here for $200 – just enough money to spend in the titty bar afterwards. He agreed and in front of Tim, Tim's parents and two others, we shook hands on that deal, spelt out very clearly. But even as he shook I had a bad feeling – it was a light shake, not genuine. I did the race, we did OK. When the time came for Tim to do the next race Goldsborough told him he wanted $10,000 deposited in his bank account for accident damage, which was not the deal we'd agreed to. Shame on him. That's what finally turned me off driving. Since then I've concentrated on my work at the racing school.

Even though I arrived in America as a road racing European, I did kind of become Americanised. I even began watching NASCAR on TV! And actually that led me to the first hero I'd ever had – Dale Earnhardt. I'd never had a hero before, even as a kid. I admired Gilles Villeneuve the F1 driver, but I was a driver on the way up then, so I never considered him a hero. But watching the NASCAR races as just a punter I really began to understand why Earnhardt had such a huge following. He had everybody scared of him, and that's the way it should be. Whenever the other guys saw him in their mirrors, they knew they had a problem. My kids grew up with Earnhardt as their hero too.

A few years ago I was driving in the Daytona 24 Hours, and so were Earnhardt and Kyle Petty, another top NASCAR driver. We were all in different classes so weren't racing directly against each other, but my kids thought it was a massive deal that I was in the same race as Earnhardt. We were chatting to Kyle in the paddock and the first thing my middle son, Taylor, asked him was could he get Earnhardt's autograph! Me and my older boy T.J. just looked at each other, embarrassed, and I muttered under my breath to Taylor, 'Dumb ass'. It's a sort of long-running joke between us because Taylor will never admit when he's done something wrong. So I say 'Dumb ass' under my breath just loud enough for him to hear. He then says, 'Hey, I'm not a dumb ass', and I say loudly, 'I never said you were a dumb ass', then mutter 'dumb ass' under my breath again. Kyle Petty is a really classy, nice man and he took it all in his stride and said, 'Sure Taylor. I'll come by tomorrow and take you over to meet him.' At that, Taylor had a huge smile on his face and said: 'Who's the dumb ass now?'

While I was waiting to go on track for practice in my Porsche, Earnhardt was in front of me in a yellow Corvette, racing in a higher class for more modified cars. I said to the mechanics over the radio, 'I'm going to pass Earnhardt,' just for fun, just to be able to say I'd done it. It was a really cold day and as we took off I dived down his inside into the hairpin and because the tyres were so cold I got a bit tweaked up and nearly sideswiped him. But I got through OK then looked in my mirrors and he was spinning. Oooh shit, I'd just nearly taken out Earnhardt on an out-lap of practice!

Kyle was as good as his word and took the boys to meet Earnhardt in his motorhome. For about the only time in their lives they were speechless. There was a possibility of me racing one of Earnhardt's Grand National stock cars. He'd said all I had to do was come up with the running expenses and I could do any one of the last three races. It was about $10,000 and I didn't find the money, because my pride wouldn't let me ask for money to race when I'd always been paid to race. I wish I'd just borrowed it because I'm pretty sure it could have changed my life.

But the life I have is pretty good. Can always be better, but pretty good. I'm now one of the core instructors at Mid Ohio. I especially enjoy our corporate days and our teen defensive driving programmes, where we teach kids of fifteen years upwards, in preparation for their driving on the roads. When I get a letter from them or their parents a few months later, saying that going through the school probably saved their lives, I get a feeling like I've won a race.

Brian Till has worked alongside Tommy as an instructor at Mid Ohio since the mid-90s. He once – only once – raced against him in Indy Lights. It was at Detroit in '91 and he put Tommy in the wall as they fought over third place. 'I didn't know Tommy then,' Till explains, 'but he just said: "Well, I guess you wanted third place more than me. I've finished third lots of times," which I thought was kind of cool.

'Bit since then I've come to know him very well. What amazes me about him as an instructor is just how adaptable he is. We run the whole gamut of instruction here, from corporate "Let's have some fun" days to serious coaching of young talent. Tommy has a great eye for talent and he will spend time with the young upcoming guys, very earnestly passing on his experience, working very conscientiously with them and really making a big difference. Then the next day he'll be doing a corporate day and he'll just be a ball of laughs. He just has to walk into a room and he's funny – if he wants to be. The demands are so different and yet he's so very good at both.

'He doesn't hit it off with everyone. After all, he's incapable of holding a thought in – if he thinks it, he says it and some people don't take to that. But others love it.

'In terms of working with the young guys, if he thinks back to his own career he was very successful very quickly and that was for a reason. He also knows his front-line career came to a premature end – and there were reasons for that too. He

can pass the good along and recognise where it might go wrong too and try to prevent it happening. We all feel we've had unfinished business as racing drivers but Tommy really was a special talent, just one of those guys that just needed full throttle and who could take care of everything else. But much as he could have had a greater career, he still achieved a hell of a lot considering he started from nothing – and I think he's come to terms with that over the years and grown into the role he has here.

'He's been given more responsibility now and he's flourishing with it and I don't think 'saviour' would be too strong a word for what the school has given him, considering how low he had got. And that's a side of him that not many people see. They see the great fun guy, the little guy with the big character that makes everyone laugh. But amid all the humour there's a lot of sadness in his story, a lot of struggle, and it's great to see him now making a success of his life.'

It's a success that's still growing, as Tommy explains.

I also have my own company, where I provide coaching services either to guys just starting out or experienced guys who want to get better. This has really taken off and quite often I'm having to subcontract guys from the school.

But before setting off full throttle on this stage of his life, the helmet well and truly hung up, there were a few things he wanted to get off his chest. Hence the book.

I wanted to write this book just to tell the story straight and to demolish a few of the myths about my career. I started writing it about ten years ago, by hand. Then I lost it. Then found it again about a year later. I left it with my dentist, who showed it to his son, who loved it, but who forgot to give me it back. So I started writing it again. I spoke to a few people about it, including my friend, David Kennedy, who told Mark Hughes, who called me – and here we are.

I wanted to write a funny book, which it was at first. But then it got harder to keep coming up with the funny stuff. The reality of it wouldn't go away. Some of the stuff in here has taken me twenty years to get to grips with, and it all came flooding out as I began to write about it: the struggles to start in Ireland, the crashes every weekend, trying to figure out how to get the money to fix the car, fixing it, trying to get the money to go to the races, crashing again, trying to get the money to fix it again ...

After instructing all week at Mid Ohio I'd see the SCCA race cars lining up waiting to go out on track and I'd shudder at the thought of all that work and energy. For what? The emotion of my own career would come out. I got it out my system a little with an old Mazda Miata race car that I use for training or for my kids or any friends that want to borrow it. I built it myself, roll cage and all, came to appreciate how much things cost after years of getting them free. But still I hate going to a racetrack unless I have reason to be there.

A couple of years ago I went to the F1 race at Indianapolis and met up with Gary Anderson and Mark Hughes who were working there. We met up the night before, a bunch of us went out to dinner and it was great, just like old times. Next day we went to the track, had breakfast, met some of my old friends from years ago, including Gerhard Berger. We were all sitting around laughing our asses off. I was having a great time but then Mark and Gary had to go off and do their stuff. Gary sent me down to the team Midland, where his daughter worked, the idea being that I could hang out there until meeting up with them again at lunchtime. But I only managed to stay there about fifteen minutes before I began feeling very uncomfortable on my own. I had a little panic attack, no idea why, and had to get out of there. I went to my car in the parking lot and stayed there until lunch. Then I met Gary and Mark and was fine again. But that's what racetracks do to me. I've more than once parked my car at a track, begun walking towards the paddock then have had to turn around and go back out. As I drive out of there a wave of happiness comes over me. Then I go home and watch it on TV!

There's a lot of emotion tied up in my career and writing the book has released some of it, but some of it got stirred up again – stuff I thought I'd got over. This is particularly true of my McLaren test. Tony Vandungen's tale of the throttle reopened old wounds. But life is too short, really. Even if that tale is true, I can forgive McLaren, Tyler Alexander etc. In fact, I have a nine-year-old son who is the best driver I've ever seen. The only difference between me and him is he listens. If Ron Dennis does for him what he did for Lewis Hamilton, I'm happy to call it quits!

I hope you've enjoyed my story.